Portfolios
in
Teacher
Education

Maureen McLaughlin
East Stroudsburg State University of Pennsylvania
East Stroudsburg, Pennsylvania

MaryEllen Vogt
California State University, Long Beach
Long Beach, California

International Reading Association
800 Barksdale Road, PO Box 8139
Newark, DE 19714–8139, USA

P9-CKV-410

Corban College Library
5000 Deer Park Drive SE
Salem, OR 97317-9392
WITHDRAWN

IRA BOARD OF DIRECTORS

Richard T. Vacca, Kent State University, Kent, Ohio, *President* • John J. Pikulski, University of Delaware, Newark, Delaware, *President-Elect* • Kathryn A. Ransom, Illinois State University, Springfield, Illinois, *Vice President* • Richard L. Allington, University at Albany–SUNY, Albany, New York • James F. Baumann, National Reading Research Center, University of Georgia, Athens, Georgia • John Elkins, University of Queensland, St. Lucia, Queensland, Australia • Yetta M. Goodman, University of Arizona, Tucson, Arizona • James V. Hoffman, The University of Texas–Austin, Austin, Texas • Kathleen Stumpf Jongsma, Northern Independent School District, San Antonio, Texas • John W. Logan, Northbrook School District 27, Northbrook, Illinois • Lesley M. Morrow, Rutgers University, New Brunswick, New Jersey • Barbara J. Walker, Montana State University–Billings, Billings, Montana • Alan E. Farstrup, Executive Director

The International Reading Association attempts, through its publications, to provide a forum for a wide spectrum of opinions on reading. This policy permits divergent viewpoints without implying the endorsement of the Association.

Acknowledgment
We gratefully acknowledge the assistance of our editor, Matt Baker.
MM & MEV

Director of Publications   Joan M. Irwin
Assistant Director of Publications   Wendy Lapham Russ
Senior Editor   Christian A. Kempers
Associate Editor   Matthew W. Baker
Assistant Editor   Janet S. Parrack
Editorial Assistant   Cynthia C. Sawaya
Association Editor   David K. Roberts
Production Department Manager   Iona Sauscermen
Graphic Design Coordinator   Boni Nash
Design Consultant   Larry F. Husfelt
Electronic Publishing Supervisor   Wendy A. Mazur
Electronic Publishing Specialist   Anette Schütz-Ruff
Electronic Publishing Specialist   Cheryl J. Strum

Photo Credits   Maureen McLaughlin, pp. 5, 93; MaryEllen Vogt, p. 23

Copyright 1996 by the International Reading Association, Inc.
All rights reserved. No part of this publication may be reproduced or transmitted in any form or by any means, electronic or mechanical, including photocopy, or any informational storage and retrieval system, without permission from the publisher.

Library of Congress Cataloging in Publication Data
McLaughlin, Maureen.
    Portfolios in teacher education / Maureen McLaughlin, MaryEllen Vogt.
        p.   cm.
    Includes bibliographical references.
    1. Portfolios in education—United States.   2. Universities and colleges—United States—Examinations—Education.   3. Teachers—Training of—United States.   I. Vogt, MaryEllen.   II. Title.
LB1728.M35   1996   96-41258
378.1'6—dc20
ISBN 0-87207-150-2

108129

For Thomas James Burke of Rose Hill, Pennsylvania; his wife, Anne; and their children Elizabeth, Mary, Ann, James, and Thomas Joseph.

MM

For Dr. Wendell H. Bragonier, the consummate teacher. Whether at the kitchen blackboard, in a seventh-grade math class, Iowa State botany lab, or the graduate school at Colorado State, he has been my inspiration and model.

MEV

CONTENTS

FOREWORD

SOME YEARS AGO, back when portfolio assessment was more talked about than done, I was asked to present a keynote address on authentic assessment at a local reading council. I recall standing in front of 150 teachers extolling the benefits and possibilities of portfolio assessment in elementary and secondary schools—listing principles and offering suggestions for exactly how these teachers could revolutionize assessment in their classrooms. When all of a sudden, I heard a voice in my head, talking even as I continued to do my presentation: "Whoa! Wait a minute here, Martha. *You* don't use portfolio assessment in your classes; you have some nerve telling these teachers to change their practice when you haven't changed yours!" It was a moment of considerable internal turmoil; I'd not faced this important and significant fact before.

That particular moment was just prior to the beginning of a semester, but the message in it was too dramatic to ignore. I simply could not continue to assign projects and give midterm and final exams if my own assessment practice was to be in any way commensurate with my beliefs. So, I did the only thing possible: I held my nose and jumped right on in to the deep and murky waters of portfolio assessment. I didn't do it exactly right that first semester, but right enough to convince me that I must continue. And I have continued over these years—refining and changing and tweaking the process along the way.

Portfolios in Teacher Education is a trailblazing text, one in which we, as teacher educators, are challenged to apply in our own classroom assessment practice parallel to the assessment practice we encourage preservice and in-service teachers to use. I particularly like the manner in which student teachers' and teachers' voices share equally with the voices of the authors in this text. First we hear one voice, then another, then the first voice, then another—the effect is a sort of call-and-refrain that rings pleasantly true.

Important also is the progression of the text from theory base to practice and then to possibilities ("Promise"). Critical in this progression is that McLaughlin and Vogt move the discussion beyond the boundaries of classroom walls. Right now—right at this very moment—teacher education and graduate reading programs all over the United States are struggling to define and put in place the means for guiding students' development of program and professional portfolios. I think it fitting and necessary that a text such as this acknowledge and address these broader arenas for portfolio development.

Another reason I like this book is the breadth and depth of Part II, "Practice," because in it the authors provide a strong framework for designing, using, and evaluating portfolios in university classes. The emphasis throughout this section remains clearly on self-reflection, making the point repeatedly that student teachers and teachers alike are enriched by their ability to reflect on what they are thinking and doing in classrooms. This serves to focus us—to remind us of the "big picture," the important assumptions underlying assessment itself. That the authors have done this while remaining utterly practical and savvy with respect to the realities of assessment and evaluation in teacher education and graduate reading programs is, I think, remarkable.

Portfolios in Teacher Education is a strong scaffold for anyone wanting to try, or get better at, portfolio assessment. What Maureen McLaughlin and MaryEllen Vogt have done in this text is lower the diving board so that, for all of us, holding our nose and jumping on in to portfolio assessment is a much safer bet.

Martha Rapp Ruddell
Sonoma State University
Rohnert Park, California

INTRODUCTION

THE EDUCATIONAL PROCESS is one of continual change. Literacy instruction now focuses on the individual reader and writer, and learning is viewed as a dynamic, strategic process (Harrison, 1996). This constructivist perspective encompasses readers and writers at all levels and promotes congruent, authentic assessment of performance.

As teacher educators, we believe that our students not only need to learn about these current instructional methods, but they also must experience them. Portfolio assessment is now viewed as an element of best practice for prospective teachers in both elementary and secondary education. Therefore, we are "practicing what we preach" by using portfolios in teacher education courses, thus encouraging our students to effectively integrate this assessment innovation into their own teaching practices.

Our purpose in writing this book is to assist teacher educators in implementing portfolio assessment. We hope that readers will be able to modify our ideas for their own teaching as they incorporate the use of portfolios in undergraduate and graduate teacher education programs. Further, we address portfolio assessment in contexts including admission to teacher education programs, student teaching, interviews, and inservice teacher evaluation.

This book is organized into three parts. Part I, "Theory," explores the theoretical tenets underpinning portfolio assessment and the decisions teacher educators must make when moving from traditional means of evaluating student learning to using portfolios. Chapter 1 explains how current assessment practices have evolved. Chapter 2 discusses how we planned the portfolio process for our university methods courses.

Part II, "Practice," introduces the portfolio process, offers examples of student work, discusses the role of self-reflection, and addresses conference and evaluation issues, including reliability and validity. Chapter 3 describes how this type of assessment is introduced to students; Chapter 4 suggests ways to develop student reflectivity, including the creation of personal literacy histories. Chapter 5 offers examples of rationale statements and excerpts from students' portfolio submissions, and Chapter 6 describes how the portfolios are evaluated. Chapter 7 relates student reactions to the use of portfolios,

1

and Chapter 8 describes the implementation of portfolios in graduate courses and the outcomes of their use.

Part III, "Promise," offers suggestions for how portfolios can be used in other university contexts and explores implications for the portfolio process. Chapter 9 addresses portfolio use in university admissions, teacher education program admissions, student teaching, job interviews, and inservice teacher evaluation. Chapter 10 describes what we have learned as a result of our portfolio experiences and contemplates the future of performance assessment.

The appendixes offer additional background about the portfolio process. Appendix A is a glossary of terms developed to facilitate readers' understanding of innovative assessment practices. It includes terminology relating to portfolio assessment and terms that emerge from the broader theoretical assessment framework. Appendix B includes our course syllabi; examples of student evaluation forms are found in Appendix C; Appendix D features additional examples of student performances; and Appendix E includes a bibliography of suggested readings.

Each chapter opens with a unique excerpt from our students' portfolio submissions. Additional examples of performances are found in chapter text and Appendix D. These pieces were created by undergraduate and graduate students, and each represents partial evidence submitted to show they were working toward a particular learning goal. We chose to include excerpts rather than the entire portfolio because of the length of portfolio submissions. The student work demonstrates the degree of self-reflection, creativity, diversity, and synthesis that results from portfolio implementation.

Additionally, throughout the text, we discuss important issues such as student evaluations, university regulations regarding examinations, and concerns about time. Although we believe that portfolio assessment offers insights into student learning we never experienced with more traditional methods, we also are clearly aware of the time constraints and other demands in teacher educators' lives. We hope our suggestions will allay concerns about the process.

When we first began discussing using portfolios as the primary means of assessing our students, we were enroute to an educational conference, where we were presenting a session on portfolio assessment. For us, the dialogue has continued throughout the portfolio process. We have inferred from our ongoing exchange of ideas that peer support is a critical factor when implementing innovations in assessment at the university level, just as it is in school districts.

Beyond our mutual support, we express thanks to our colleagues for their contributions to the field of assessment and evaluation. Further, we are grateful to our students for their sense of adventure and openness. Their insights and performances continually amaze us. We are convinced that portfolio assessment encourages students to learn and understand in greater depth, and we hope other teacher educators discover the same as they explore this fascinating process.

PART ONE

THEORY

CHAPTER ONE

What Is Literacy?

Literacy is not a hook
on every sound pronounced.
It's not a drill
of a repeated skill,
nor a hammer
into blocks of grammar.

Literacy is fun.
It's reading by flashlight
or out in the sun.

It's news about the president,
the weather, the Superbowl, TV stars,
and even Calvin and Hobbes
in the Sunday Times.

It's a recipe for cookies,
a shopping list, notes on the refrigerator,
a secret Valentine,
birthday cards and letters
from long ago friends.

It's traveling to foreign lands
without leaving your bed.
It's laughing and crying
with characters, heroes, and best friends.

It's an atlas of the world,
street signs, treasure hunts,
manuals, instructions, guides,
and directions on medicine bottles
so you won't get lost.

Literacy is most
a map of the human heart
of who we are and all that we can be.

Kate M. Chong
*This poem by Chong, a student
in the secondary reading methods class,
is excerpted from her personal literacy history.*

Moving Along the
Assessment Continuum

O NE OF THE greatest challenges teacher educators face today is keeping abreast of innovations in the field. We read, research, and write about current theories and how they affect not only teaching in elementary and secondary schools, but also instruction at the university level. It is important to acknowledge the relation between these two institutions because school systems and university education programs are inextricably linked.

We educate those who choose to become teachers. In addition to our obligations to the universities, we spend time teaching in the public schools, serve as consultants to them, engage in collaborative efforts involving university and public school students, and interact with classroom teachers for research purposes. Consequently, we strive to teach what is current practice as well as innovations that may be in place when our preservice teachers have their own classrooms. One of our focuses is the assessment and evaluation of student performance. This chapter provides the background and theoretical underpinnings for our move from traditional evaluation procedures to more authentic means of measuring our students' progress and achievement.

TRADITIONAL ASSESSMENT PERSPECTIVES

Historically, educational evaluation has consisted of administering periodic quizzes, reports, or tests. In many cases these have been the bases of report card grades in elementary and secondary schools as well as course grades at the university level. In the United States, these traditional evaluations frequently have been complemented by standardized tests such as the Stanford Achievement Test in public schools, the Scholastic Assessment Test (SAT), formerly known as the Scholastic Aptitude Test, for admission to universities, and the National Teachers' Examination (NTE) in university schools of education.

The results of these tests have been used for diverse purposes including student placement and accountability. In public schools such scores have been mandated by federal or state programs, and colleges and universities have required them for admission to both the institutions themselves as well as specific programs. Neill and Medina (1989) estimate that more than 105 million standardized tests are administered annually to 39.8 million students in the United States.

Concerns about assessment and evaluation practices became evident in the United States in the 1970s and early 1980s with the advent of minimum competency testing in elementary and secondary schools (McLaughlin, 1986). These measures were largely the result of the public sector's demands for accountability. Community members were concerned because many students holding high school diplomas did not possess the competencies needed to enter the workforce. This prompted many states to develop tests to measure students' minimum skills in reading and mathematics. If students did not meet certain predetermined required scores, they were offered additional instructional assistance in the area of demonstrated need. At the time these programs appeared beneficial, though gains in student achievement occurred primarily for low achieving students (Linn, 1995).

There were also other concerns with minimum competency testing: students' minimum competencies were frequently measured on the basis of just one test; many of these measures were structured similarly to standardized tests; questions arose about validity and the alignment of curriculum, instruction, and assessment; and the minimum competency programs had too restricted a view of the educational process, focusing on students' ability to perform at the minimum level rather than on each child's maximum potential. We now realize that the focus should have been on each child's maximum potential rather than on a minimum level of competency.

While the public schools in the United States were using minimum competency measures, universities continued to evaluate students' abilities by requiring SATs for admission to undergraduate programs, NTEs to exit undergraduate education programs, and the Graduate Record Examination (GRE) and Miller's Analogies Test for entrance to graduate programs. While widely acceptable for a time, these evaluations have provoked questions concerning what the tests tell us about student learning. None appears to offer information about an individual student's reasoning processes, an important factor in the constructivist perspective.

It has become increasingly evident that the results of traditional standardized tests are not telling teachers all we need to know about student progress in learning. Characterized by pencil and paper formats, multiple-choice responses, time-restricted completion, and scoring by the testing company, these tests offer no direct evidence of how students engage in the learning process (McLaughlin & Kennedy, 1993). Other issues associated with standardized testing include the following: (1) they are based on an outdated model of literacy; (2) they frequently promote achievement but exclude development; (3) they lack coordination with instructional goals and are easily misinterpreted and misused; (4) they prohibit the use of learning strategies; (5) they serve as poor predictors of individual performance; and (6) they categorize and label students (Winograd, Paris, & Bridge, 1991; Wolf, 1989; Worthen, 1993).

INNOVATIONS IN ASSESSMENT

In the 1990s, Pikulski (1990) encouraged educators to focus assessment and evaluation efforts on lessening the misuses of standardized tests, improving existing tests, and developing alternative means of assessment. Demands for new approaches suggested a shift from fixed-response, machine-scorable tests to the evaluation of performance tasks that required open-ended, student-constructed responses (Linn, 1995). Shepard (1989) and Valencia (1990) offered views of assessment as an authentic, multifaceted process. Paris (1991) delineated the need to align curriculum, instruction, and assessment. This demand for a new approach was coupled with an increasing awareness that in real-life situations, such as the medical and industrial fields, evaluation is performance based.

What has emerged is assessment that is authentic in nature, offers multiple indicators of student progress, encourages students to take an active role in their learning, affords teachers new roles in the assessment process, and encourages students to demonstrate what they know in ways that encompass their personal learning styles (Vogt, McLaughlin, & Ruddell, 1993). This assessment, congruent with current theories of learning and teaching, is predicated on the following interrelated and integrated theories:

- Constructivism: Learners make sense of their world by connecting what they know and have experienced with what they are learning. They construct meaning through these connections when educators pose relevant problems, encourage student inquiry, structure learning activities around primary concepts, value students' points of view, and assess student learning so that it is contextualized by the teaching (Brooks & Brooks, 1993; Short & Burke, 1996).

- Social Negotiation and the Zone of Proximal Development: Students construct understandings and interpretations when learning is scaffolded by more experienced people. The Zone of Proximal Development represents the difference between what learners are able to do alone and what they can do when they have the assistance and support of others. Social interaction between learners thus enhances meaning construction. This is evidenced in classrooms where teachers and professors plan activities that incorporate multiple opportunities for students to socially interact with others (Dixon-Krauss, 1996; Swafford, 1996; Vygotsky, 1987).

- Schema-Based Learning Development: Learning takes place when new information is added to previously acquired knowledge. The more experience learners have with a particular topic, the easier it is for them to make connections between what they know and what they are learning (Anderson, 1995; Rumelhart, 1994). Educators assist students in making these connections and in building background knowledge for those who may lack prior experience with what is being learned.

- The Reflective Practitioner: Teachers learn to teach and improve their teaching through ongoing reflection about their practices and students. These reflections develop understandings and insights that can lead to better ways of teaching (Schon, 1987).

Portfolio assessment incorporates these theoretical tenets because it (1) requires performances that demonstrate students' meaning construction; (2) is collaborative, necessitating interactions and support from others; (3) nurtures students as inquirers; (4) demonstrates students' progress over time, valuing increasing knowledge and application of what is learned; and (5) requires students to self-reflect and self-assess, promoting reflectivity about practice.

Portfolio assessment refers to both a *process* and a *construct*. The *process* involves students and teachers working collaboratively to create a portfolio that will be both multidimensional and dynamic (Valencia, 1990). The *construct*, such as a folder, binder, box, or notebook, is where the assessments are collected. Since its inception, many varied recommendations about portfolio development have been offered (Au, 1993; Flood & Lapp, 1989; Tierney, Carter, & Desai, 1991), and increasing numbers of elementary and secondary teachers are implementing them. Portfolios capture and capitalize on each student's maximum potential and they encourage diverse ways to assess learning and growth not typically found in formal or standardized testing (Ruddell & Ruddell, 1995).

As portfolio assessment in elementary, middle, and secondary schools has become more prevalent, there has been a growing need for preservice and inservice teachers to augment their awareness of innovations in the assessment process. However, just learning about the philosophy inherent in an assessment practice is not sufficient; we believe that if teacher educators expect students to emerge as knowledgeable teachers able to develop portfolios with their students, they must first experience portfolio assessment for themselves. An increasing interest in this notion is supported by others in the fields of literacy and teacher education (Anderson, 1995; Ford, 1994; Heiden, 1996; Mosenthal, Daniels, & Mekkelsen, 1992; Ohlhausen, Perkins, & Jones, 1993; Roehler, 1995; Ruddell, 1995; Stowell, 1993). Discussions among teacher educators at recent national and state education conferences in the United States have explored the value of portfolios in teacher education, the processes used to guide portfolio development, managing portfolios for evaluation of student performance, the use of portfolios as objects of inquiry and reflection, and the role of portfolios as alternative assessments situated in the university.

Designing a System

Our primary focus was to design an authentic assessment system that would enable us to see how our students engage in learning while they are immersed in the portfolio process. We soon realized that this would involve the following:

- learning about innovative perspectives,

- choosing ideas that work in our contexts,

- holding discussions with peers and administrators,

- interacting with students to ensure the assessment system would be collaborative in nature, and

- aligning the innovations with university grading policies.

As we began studying suggested innovations, it became clear that having a shared understanding of the language of assessment would be a critical precursor to implementation. For example, it was important to know the distinction between the terms *assessment*—the gathering of information regarding students' learning—and *evaluation*—making judgments about students' learning (Ferrara & McTighe, 1992).

It also was evident that although *alternative assessment* refers to nontraditional modes, it still encompasses considerable latitude. Tierney (1996) describes it as "having to do with a way of teaching, testing, and knowing that is aligned with a set of values that are different than what has been and still is espoused by most educational reformers" (p. 3). *Performance assessment*, a type of alternative assessment, asks students to demonstrate what they have learned. It shows how they engage in the learning process as well as how they apply their knowledge. Performance assessment is not new to education; it was "common in many 19th century and early progressive schools but became less important with the rise of standardized testing" (Viechnicki et al., 1993, p. 371). Another term that was important to us in our attempts to design an assessment system was *authentic assessment*: engaging students in tasks that are grounded in instruction, personally meaningful, and situated in real-world experiences (McLaughlin & Kennedy, 1993). When we clarified our understandings of these various terms and had a common focus and commitment to implementing authentic assessment practices congruent with what we were teaching our students, we were ready to begin. (For a complete glossary of assessment terms, see Appendix A.)

A FINAL THOUGHT

After reviewing the current literature and discussing portfolios with university colleagues, six principles became essential to us. We knew that our students' assessment and evaluation must incorporate

- *performance*, to encourage students to apply their knowledge;

- *portfolios*, to offer students a comprehensive, reflective record of their learning;

- *reliability*, to provide students with goals toward which to work, while accommodating multiple indicators of their progress;

- *validity*, to afford students a clear understanding that assessment and instruction are inextricably linked;

- *collaboration*, to promote both professor-student and student-student interaction; and

- *reflectivity*, to foster student reasoning and self-assessment.

These central principles guided our conceptualizing, implementing, and subsequent revising of the portfolio assessment process. Chapter 2 describes the steps we took to implement this type of assessment.

Chapter Two

Why wait for the future when you can drive tomorrow's literacy vehicle today?

Introducing our newest model:

Constructivism

Loaded with standard features:

Vibrant turn signal indicators and easy to use horn for important *social negotiation*

Environmentally friendly, emissions free electric memory fuel cells provide world knowledge to the engine

Sensitive metacognitive navigation computer monitors your progress and helps you find your way

Advanced cerebral cortex engine provides plenty of power, to take you anywhere you want to go

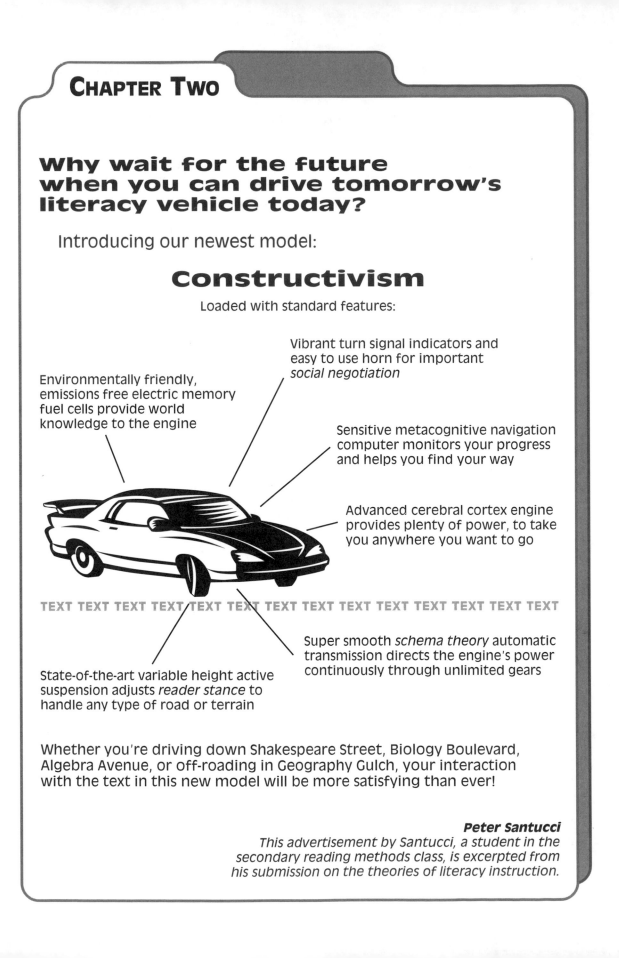

TEXT TEXT TEXT TEXT TEXT TEXT TEXT TEXT TEXT TEXT TEXT TEXT TEXT TEXT

Super smooth *schema theory* automatic transmission directs the engine's power continuously through unlimited gears

State-of-the-art variable height active suspension adjusts *reader stance* to handle any type of road or terrain

Whether you're driving down Shakespeare Street, Biology Boulevard, Algebra Avenue, or off-roading in Geography Gulch, your interaction with the text in this new model will be more satisfying than ever!

Peter Santucci
This advertisement by Santucci, a student in the secondary reading methods class, is excerpted from his submission on the theories of literacy instruction.

ALIGNING THEORY AND PRACTICE

A S WITH ALL innovations, working knowledge of theory leads to contemplation of utility. Consequently, context became a critical factor as we began thinking about how we might implement the use of portfolios in our elementary and secondary reading methods classes. Creating a link among curriculum, instruction, and assessment was our guiding principle as we pondered how best to use the information from current theoretical perspectives about portfolios. This chapter details what we experienced as we aligned theory with our teaching and provides an overview of the portfolio process we propose.

GETTING STARTED

From the outset, we considered our teaching to be current, yet we relied on more traditional means of assessment for assigning university-mandated letter grades. Throughout the semesters we had taught at the university level we collected grades for lesson and unit plans, projects, journal abstracts, quizzes, midterms, and final examinations. This was congruent with common practice in teacher education as well as university regulations regarding student evaluation. Though our universities have slightly different evaluation policies, we were both required to issue letter grades, have a minimum number of graded samples per student, meet for a final examination, and keep grade distributions relatively consistent with other courses in our departments. Thus, while we have a degree of academic freedom, we must follow university practices in regard to the evaluation of our students.

We soon learned, however, that as our respective course curricula moved away from traditional basal and textbook instruction to more integrated language arts approaches, our methods of evaluation no longer seemed compatible with our teaching. This concern about the incongruity between teaching and assessment has been voiced by others (Stowell & Tierney, 1995). How could we teach one way and assess in a different way? How could we tell our classes to assess their eventual students with portfolios, yet evaluate our students' own performance through traditional means? At this point, even though we had university constraints, we knew it was time for a change.

DEVELOPING GOALS

Our initial planning needed to be situated within the university classroom, although our respective contexts differed. One of us taught elementary reading methods in an undergraduate teacher certification program, and the other taught secondary reading methods in a postbaccalaureate fifth-year credential program. We wondered if this difference would affect our assessment methods but found our initial questions about the process were the same: What will the portfolios look like? How will students react to them? Should we give exams or will portfolio data be enough? We soon discovered that we needed a viable plan for developing, organizing, and managing this innovative assessment, regardless of the literacy courses we taught.

We began with our respective course curricula formulated from state frameworks, credentialing standards, and standard course outlines. Course objectives, which had been numerous, were soon rethought, clustered within global course "goals," and stated in terms of the students' performance. These goals have served as the focal point of our assessment. For example, the elementary reading methods class includes the following goals:

> By the end of the course of study, students will be able to demonstrate knowledge and application of
>
> - contemporary theories of literacy instruction;
> - authentic literature and its role in the instructional process;
> - curriculum, instruction, and assessment; and
> - current developments in literacy education.

For the secondary methods course, the following goals were outlined:

> By the end of the course of study, students will be able to demonstrate knowledge and application of
>
> - the history of elementary and secondary literacy instruction and the relationship between that history and their own literacy development;
> - current theories and principles that support literacy and learning;
> - the interrelation between assessment and instruction in secondary content areas;

- assessment and instruction of one or more students who need assistance in any or all of the following areas: reading, writing, study skills, or specific content area learning; and
- interesting and appealing trade books for middle and secondary school students.

These goals have been refined over the semesters we have used portfolios, and they represent the most salient curriculum areas we teach.

Up to this point, we developed the goals for our courses. Additionally, we facilitated discussion about them, set due dates and format requirements for the evidence, and eventually assigned each student a letter grade. Even though students had considerable choice and flexibility about the evidence they submitted for each goal, we determined the parameters. To offer greater authenticity, give students more involvement in the goal-setting process, and make the assessment more continuous and ongoing (Valencia, Hiebert, & Afflerbach, 1994), we added another goal:

> Students will set and work toward fulfilling a personal literacy-related goal.

In this process, what students select as their goal is as important as the evidence they submit to demonstrate their progress in meeting it.

We believe that both classroom teachers and university professors must begin the portfolio process by creating a link among curriculum, instruction, and assessment. Creating learning goals helps students see from the onset that teaching is situated within a curriculum and that assessment of students must be linked directly to instructional goals derived from that curriculum. Establishing this connection also results in greater reliability for the portfolio process (Gellman, 1992–1993). (See Chapter 6 for a discussion of reliability issues.)

DETERMINING INDICATORS

After we established learning goals, we had to decide what students would do with them. At first, we both took an unstructured approach by suggesting that students submit whatever evidence they chose for each goal. After the first semester, we discovered that our students found the lack of structure very frustrating. They wanted and needed some guidelines, especially because the process was unfamiliar and somewhat intimidating. But this led to another dilemma: Is it possible to clearly communicate expectations without overly controlling the process? If the process has structure, will this diminish student choice and reflection? In response to these concerns, we brainstormed a number of *possibilities* of evidence for each goal. Offering these possibilities in the course syllabi assists students in making decisions about their evidence while ensuring the integrity of the portfolio process is maintained.

For the elementary course goal dealing with developing an understanding of current theories of literacy instruction, we include possibilities such as the following:

- Create your literacy history, citing the presence or absence of teaching from a particular perspective.
- Compare and contrast the role of constructivism in various models of reading.
- Interview a teacher.
- Observe a classroom and reflect upon the constructivist nature of the lesson.
- Plan a literacy lesson from a particular perspective or redesign a plan you created earlier to include the particular theory.

For the secondary course goal concerning the theories and principles that support literacy instruction, possibilities include those listed here:

- Reflect upon how you might teach your content from a constructivist perspective, giving specific ideas for instruction.
- Plan or revise a content lesson to incorporate theoretically sound strategies and activities.
- Ask teachers whether they teach from a theoretical perspective, and if so, which one.
- Observe a classroom lesson and attempt to determine the teacher's theoretical underpinnings.
- Reflect on how you were taught content subjects, and give examples of how teachers incorporated constructivist theory into their teaching.

These portfolio possibilities reduce students' anxiety and serve as a starting point for them to generate their own ideas. Each possibility is broad enough to allow for individual interpretation, creativity, and variation. Further, time in class is given regularly to discuss all kinds of possibilities, which helps answer the question, "How much is enough to include?" Students begin to realize that "enough" depends on the nature of the evidence they wish to submit.

THE PORTFOLIO CONSTRUCT

Because there are many students in our classes and we must transport the portfolios, we needed to consider how to contain students' material. Three-ring binders or bracketed pocket folders work well. Posters, videos, and models are submitted separately. We have found it helpful to give guidance about the type of portfolio to use and also provide specific information about format and organization.

RATIONALE STATEMENTS

Reflection is a critical aspect of the portfolio process. In elementary and secondary schools, it is often seen in an entry slip or "letter to the reader" that is attached to each piece of evidence that goes into the portfolio. In our classes, students write *rationale statements*, reflecting on why a particular goal is important to them as teachers and explaining how the evidence relates to the goal. The rationale statements promote reflection, encourage individual goal-setting, reduce ambiguity, and guide the reader through the portfolio. (See Chapter 4 for a discussion of reflectivity.)

EVALUATION CRITERIA

When we created our course evaluation policies, we again needed to consider university regulations. We thought about including quizzes, midterms, and final exams because they are familiar and have been generally accepted as a means of evaluating student performance. In fact, at one of our universities, a final examination is required in all courses and exemption from the policy must be received in writing from the Dean of the school.

After much contemplation, we decided to forego administering examinations. We have discovered that portfolios provide ample evidence of student understanding and application of course content. In accordance with university policy, we have determined that multiple items for evaluation and criteria that are detailed in the syllabus satisfy university grading requirements. After using portfolios for eight semesters, we have never encountered any challenges or concerns about our grading practices. We have avoided problems, we believe, because our grading policies are clearly explained in our syllabi and because the evaluation of the portfolios is carefully structured. Since our students must maintain a minimum grade point average for their teacher education methods courses, our evaluation policies must be above reproach.

To assist students in understanding how their portfolios will be evaluated, we have established a rubric with the following descriptors:

exceptional

thorough

adequate

inadequate

Groups of students brainstorm and formulate a specific description for each of these categories at the start of each course. We have found this part of the process to be very helpful for both us and the students. (See Chapter 6 for a complete explanation of the rubric.)

PORTFOLIO PLANNERS

Using the Portfolio Planner is another critical step in the portfolio process. On this planner, students share plans for the evidence they will include in their portfolios and explain their reasoning. Planners are submitted two to three weeks prior to the portfolio due dates. We read them, hold conferences with students, and offer oral and written feedback. The planners assist students who may be confused about the process by providing early feedback about evidence they intend to submit. (See Chapter 6 for examples of the Portfolio Planner.)

THE SYLLABI

As we began to create our syllabi, we knew that the success of incorporating portfolio assessment might depend on the clarity of our directions. An overview of the portfolio process is not sufficient for students to fully understand what they are required to do, and we cannot rely on in-class explanations for all the details involved. When we first introduced portfolios, we were concerned about how students would evaluate the class at the end of the semester, especially our students' feeling fully informed of class expectations and requirements.

Both of us use current textbooks in our methods courses that explain how portfolio assessment is used in the elementary and secondary schools. Although our students will eventually understand the process when they read about it, discuss it in class, and become immersed in it, we must also ensure that at the first class meeting they understand what is expected of them. Therefore, we provide a detailed syllabus that includes all the previously mentioned components of portfolio development. It helps to ground the assessment in curriculum. We clearly state each of the learning goals in the syllabus along with a complete description of the portfolio process. (See Appendix B for course syllabi.)

A FINAL THOUGHT

Deciding to use portfolios in a teacher education course requires a number of challenging decisions about parameters, organization, and management. What a professor chooses to do will depend on the context in which he or she teaches, whether the course is undergraduate or graduate, and his or her teaching style. Some may believe this portfolio process is too structured and that students need more control. However, we feel comfortable in our approach because we tried less structure and encountered several problems, including student procrastination, submissions without a clear focus or rationale, evidence of little or no reflection, and too many items that demonstrated little evidence of student learning. So, we have continued to refine our process. However, it is important to remember that this type of assessment is situated, and each individual context should guide the development of the assessment plan.

PART TWO

PRACTICE

Western Baptist College Library

CHAPTER THREE

The Turtle

When I was little
I wrote a story
About a turtle.
I was full of self-pride
At what I had created.
I wanted to share it
With the family
But they wanted to see
The Brady Bunch
"Shh," they said,
"Wait 'til the commercial."

When they found time to read
"The Turtle"
In between the show
And the commercial,
They said, "It's good."
(Now leave us alone.)
So I crumpled up "The Turtle."
They looked at me and said,
"Why did you do that?"
Then turned to watch TV
Before the end of the commercial.

Andrea Willoughby
*This poem by Willoughby, a student in the
secondary reading methods class, is excerpted
from her personal literacy history.*

INTRODUCING PORTFOLIOS: CONCEPT AND PROCESS

PORTFOLIO ASSESSMENT IS a term that many of our students have heard but know little about. This chapter details how we introduce the portfolio process in our classes. Student acceptance is critical to the success of portfolios, and careful modeling and explanation enhances understandings and decreases anxiety about the process.

IN THE BEGINNING

The initial information we share with our students is of a very introductory nature. The concept is broached by discussing various professionals who are evaluated by performance assessment. Discussion then moves to what can be learned about people from their performances over time. Students frequently note that observers can tell what practitioners are able to do and what kind of progress is being made. This leads to talk about the history of the performer and the diversity of his or her work. When students realize that performance assessment is prevalent in other situations in life, they are better able to understand the role of performance assessment in teaching and learning. Sharing students' prior knowledge serves as the foundation for the introduction to the portfolio process and is congruent with constructivist perspectives of learning.

THE PERSONAL PORTFOLIO

To assist in further understanding, we share our personal portfolios that are structured to model ownership of the process as well as its organization and management (McLaughlin, 1995). We introduce these by talking about why and how they were created; how we decided which personal goals to address; and how the portfolios serve as evidence of our history and diversity in reflecting who we are, what we can do, and how we feel about our performances.

Pieces of evidence in these personal portfolios include a focus on family life (pictures, letters, journals, and videotapes); academics (syllabi, publications, and programs from professional presentations); and personal literacy (e-mail messages, personal correspondence, and a log of books read). It is important to note that what we are demonstrating is the *process*, from the identification of goals, to the rationale, to the selection and collection of relevant evidence.

Because we are modeling the process, we organize our portfolios in a manageable way. The portfolios are contained in a three-ring binder or pocket folder with fasteners. Goals are tabbed to ensure easy location. Each section begins with a statement of the goal, followed by our reflections that address issues such as what meaning the goal holds for us, why we value it, and how we feel about our progress toward achieving it. Next, we include the artifacts and again reflect about how each piece of evidence relates to the goal it has been selected to support. We are careful to note that many different types of evidence could support each goal, and some indicators may support more than one goal. Selection is a key facet of the portfolio process.

Modeling the process offers several benefits: (1) it allows students to see that we value what we are asking them to do; (2) it affords them an opportunity to see how a portfolio might be structured; (3) it gives both professors and students insight into the reflective process; and (4) it offers greater depth to the student-professor relationship. An additional positive outcome is the students' realization that modeling is a valuable part of instruction.

After sharing our personal portfolios, we elicit students' hopes for and concerns about the portfolio process. We address these issues in class discussions, peer sharing, and student-professor conferences throughout the semester.

Part of the sharing process also involves encouraging students to think of a personal literacy goal as an introduction to creating a course goal. To promote this, we ask students to form groups to generate personal goals relating to reading and writing. They then brainstorm indicators of how an individual could demonstrate progress toward meeting these goals. An emphasis is put on multiple, multidimensional indicators; for example, one student's literacy goal was to access the Internet in order to telecommunicate with peers during student teaching. Possible evidence suggested by the student's group included the following indicators that would demonstrate that the student is actively pursuing Internet connectivity:

- promotional information from an Internet Service Provider (ISP);
- an application for the connectivity service;
- a receipt from the ISP indicating a membership had been purchased;
- the student's e-mail address; and
- a list of fellow student teachers' e-mail addresses.

At this point, students were reminded that portfolio evidence must demonstrate *performance*. In other words, though contracting with an ISP is a start, it does not represent the actual intent of the goal—to telecommunicate. Therefore, students added the following possible pieces of evidence to their list:

- a log of e-mail messages sent and received;

- a disk (or hard copies) of e-mail messages sent to peers and others;

- a disk (or hard copies) of e-mail messages received from peers and others; and

- a written reflection about how the Internet had enriched the student's life.

We found that this brainstorming activity helps students to relate the process to their background knowledge before they transfer the portfolio strategies to specific academic goals. Besides, there is an enjoyable interaction as students share personal goals and possible evidences for achieving those goals.

Frequently, students ask to see examples of former students' portfolios. We choose not to display completed portfolios because each is unique and there is no one correct way to create them. However, we do share examples of former students' rationale statements and an accompanying piece of evidence such as a poem, cartoon, self-authored children's book, student-authored newspaper, or essay. When our students see transparencies of sample rationale statements that vary in length and style as well as accompanying evidence, they begin to understand the possibilities. These examples spark students' creativity and reduce much of the ambiguity inherent in the portfolio process.

The dynamic nature of assessment has resulted in changes in the way we introduce portfolios to our students. Wiggins (1993) notes that the redeployment of time is an important factor in portfolio use. We have found that when ample time is allotted in the early stages of using portfolios in our classes, students have less anxiety about their portfolios, have a more reasonable expectation of the time needed to complete them, and improve the overall quality of their work.

COMPARING SCHOOL AND UNIVERSITY PORTFOLIO DEVELOPMENT

While teaching the portfolio process to preservice teachers, it is important to parallel the creation of portfolios in elementary, middle, and secondary schools. This offers additional benefits to the preservice teachers because they can see the connection between the university assessment plan and the one they may use in their own classrooms.

The steps we follow to develop portfolio assessment at the university level are as follows:

1. Recognize the importance of curricular, instructional, assessment, and evaluation alignment.

2. Develop course goals.

3. Create authentic performance indicators.

4. Incorporate reflectivity.

5. Develop criteria for evaluation.

6. Correlate evaluation with the university grading system.

7. Manage the process.

8. Use assessment results.

Elementary and secondary school systems follow a very similar process. The major difference seems to be the extent of the involvement of the educational stakeholders, other than students and teachers. At the school level, parents, administrators, and community members may choose to play an active role in portfolio development. At the university, however, there is less of an emphasis on sharing portfolios with audiences other than students and professors, although many students choose to share them informally with families. Another difference involving stakeholders is that whereas both students and teachers may select evidence to be included in the portfolios at the school district level, our university students self-select their indicators. The basic tenets of portfolio development, however, are similar and parallels can be drawn in the areas of curriculum, time, alignment with required reporting methods, resistance to change, and real-life experiences.

CURRICULUM

Because the curriculum serves as the source of the course goals, an important issue is ensuring that the curriculum is thoroughly updated. This is time consuming at both the university and the elementary and secondary levels. At the university, changes in curriculum must be developed first and then approved by peers, various committees, and the administration. This can be a lengthy process. In school systems, meeting times must be arranged to afford faculty input into curricular innovation. Changes also may require administrative and school board approval.

TIME

Another shared concern at both education levels is the time that portfolios require to implement and manage. For those elementary and secondary teachers who have had experience with the process during teacher education, the time may be lessened. Still, time remains a critical factor as professors and teachers need time to

- learn about assessment innovations,

- share their knowledge with peers,

- interact with the curriculum,

- update instructional techniques,

- share assessment information with the educational stakeholders,

- explain the portfolio process to students,

- interact with students in portfolio planning,

- hold conferences with students,

- offer feedback about students' portfolios,

- align students' portfolios with the grading system, and

- use the outcomes of the process to assist in planning for future portfolio use (McLaughlin, 1995).

ALIGNMENT WITH REQUIRED REPORTING METHODS

Aligning innovative assessment procedures with traditional reporting methods is a challenging task. Holding conferences with students does ease this difficulty to some degree, but many professors and teachers using portfolios are mandated to relate the outcomes of the assessments to traditional grading systems. For example, because we both teach within state university systems, regardless of how innovative our practices are, we must correlate them to the traditional grading systems structured by California's and Pennsylvania's state university requirements. In the same way, redesigning written report cards at the school district level is a challenging experience, one that is currently underway in many districts, and one in which many of our current students may become involved.

MANDATES AND RESISTANCE TO CHANGE

We also must note that portfolios have not been mandated at the university level as they have been for school systems in various U.S. states. Whether these mandates assist or hinder teacher acceptance of portfolios is unclear.

Although numerous school districts are successfully using portfolio assessment, our students are occasionally challenged by teachers in the field about the process. They report that a few classroom teachers, most often at the high school level, have commented that portfolios are "just another educational trend." Teachers sometimes add that portfolios represent efforts at school reform but believe they are impractical and unrealistic. Overcoming these negative convictions is a challenge at both the university level and in elementary and secondary schools. We have found, however, that our students' concerns about portfolios are largely ameliorated when they become involved in the process.

EXPERIENCES IN THE FIELD

To further assist students in recognizing parallels between using portfolios in the schools and using them in teacher education programs, both our elementary and secondary preservice teachers participate in shared portfolio experiences with school children. These portfolio celebration days are held at elementary and middle schools, and they have proved beneficial in the following ways (Vogt & McLaughlin, 1995):

- Elementary and middle school children, as well as university students, gain understanding that the portfolio process is valued by others.

- Both groups of students demonstrate facility in communicating their thoughts about the assessment process to different audiences.

- The preservice teachers have the opportunity to engage in an assessment process that is situated in an environment similar to one in which they will teach.

- The school children see that learning has purpose beyond the classroom.

- As they share their respective portfolios, both the school children and the preservice teachers gain greater insight into the authentic, performance nature of the portfolio process.

A Final Thought

Although we both spend a significant amount of time modeling, discussing, and answering questions about the portfolio process, the reality is that our students' understandings develop gradually over the course of the semester. Their insights evolve as they experience planning, collecting, organizing, and completing their first portfolio submission.

CHAPTER FOUR

From as far back as I can remember, I have loved to read. I am sure part of this desire came from positive reinforcement at school and some exceptional teachers; however, I attribute my continuing interest in reading to growing up in a literacy rich environment. Both my mother and my grandfather recall my great-grandmother being a wonderful storyteller. My grandfather (age 86) attributes much of his learning to his parents' oral instruction. When he was a small boy he remembers being told stories just like I remember being read to. My mother recollects being told wonderful epic poems by my great-grandmother who had memorized them years before. Thankfully, my grandfather has carried on this tradition and is one of the best storytellers I know today.

Karlin Overlie
This passage by Overlie, a student in the elementary reading methods class, is excerpted from her personal literacy history.

CREATING SELF-REFLECTION

SELF-REFLECTION IS THE heart of portfolio assessment. It encourages students to ponder what course goals mean and contemplate their ownership of the portfolio process. It tells students that we value their thinking and affords us access to information we have never had in the past. This chapter explains how we link self-reflection to students' real-life experiences, create an atmosphere of mutual trust, and encourage our students to demonstrate their reflective abilities in their literacy histories, conferences, small-group discussion, rationale statements, and portfolio self-evaluation.

INTRODUCING SELF-REFLECTION

As with other aspects of portfolio assessment, the initial development of self-reflection is an issue of concern. Student anxiety in this area results from inexperience; they are simply not accustomed to being reflective about course work. Many cannot recall an episode in an educational context in which they have been asked to express what they think. Others can recall examples of being asked to express their thoughts in which they were told that their thinking was incorrect or not the acceptable interpretation. Providing a rationale for reflectivity is critical at this point. Students need to internalize that learning "to engage in reflective thinking and to make reflective judgments...is a central point of higher education" (King & Kitchener, 1994, p. 222). Further, students need to understand that reflectivity is "rightfully active...and calls for personal and professional transformation" (Wellington, 1991, p. 5). Students need to embrace reflectivity as a valued component of their educational experience.

Next, we remind students that reflection is a part of everyday life. We model this process by reflecting on some aspect of our own lives. Then students use their prior knowledge to reflect on an aspect of their lives. They describe their last experience with a hobby or special interest, evaluate their performance, and set a new personal goal that will help them perform better in the future (McLaughlin, 1995).

LITERACY HISTORIES

When the students feel comfortable with the concept, they reflect on another experience they have had: their literacy development. This activity invites students to examine their personal literacy journey as they create their literacy histories.

A literacy history details a person's reflections on his or her emergence into literacy, chronicling its development from earliest memory to present day (McLaughlin, 1994). Such a process personalizes the learning experience. In many cases, this leads to discussions with family members and peers and allows students to become comfortable with the process of self-reflection because it is grounded in their own experiences. This supports the view that "portfolios should be viewed as vehicles for student self-evaluation and assessment practices rooted in the life of the classroom and the world of the student" (Tierney, Carter, & Desai, 1991, p. 123).

The focus of the literacy history is the student's ability to relate prior knowledge to current experiences. This follows the reflective practitioner model, which encourages teachers to purposefully and thoughtfully analyze their instruction (Roth, 1989; Schon, 1987). Our students purposefully and thoughtfully examine their engagement in literacy, a meaningful and enlightening action for those whose life's work will focus on engaging others in the literacy process. This project makes our students aware of the factors that influence literacy and offers them the opportunity to ponder the roles they may play in their own students' literacy development (Graves, 1990). Further, as our students monitor their engagement in the literacy process, they acknowledge its dynamic nature and set new goals for themselves.

Because one of the primary goals of our methods classes is to interact with our students in ways similar to those in which they will interact with their students, we introduce and then model the concept of the literacy history.

LITERACY HISTORY PROMPTS

When sharing our literacy histories, we are careful not to limit the students' creations to what they hear from their professor. Still, throughout our years of portfolio use, students have expressed concerns about what to include. Because each literacy history is unique, we did not want to provide specific parameters, but it soon became clear that offering some direction might allay students' anxieties. Literacy histories from three semesters were studied to develop the following list of prompts (see Figure 1) to assist students in creating and organizing their thoughts.

Figure 1 Literacy History Prompts

These prompts have been developed to assist you in creating your literacy history. Please know that this is not a definitive list of questions to which you should respond, but rather a sequence of ideas to stimulate your thinking about your own literacy development. As you listen to my literacy history, you will notice that while I have chosen to include many of the ideas expressed in the prompts, I have not allowed them to restrict my thinking. Please use the same creative freedom as you record your experiences.

1. What are your earliest recollections of reading and writing?
2. Were you read to as a child?
3. Before you were able to read, did you pretend to read books? Can you remember the first time you read a book?
4. Did you read and/or write with your siblings or friends?
5. Can you recall your early writing attempts (scribbling, labeling drawings, etc.)?
6. Was a newspaper delivered to your home? Do you recall seeing others read the newspaper? Did you read the newspaper?
7. Did you subscribe to children's magazines? Did your parents or siblings have magazine subscriptions?
8. Did your parents belong to a book club? Did they maintain a personal library? Did they read for pleasure?
9. Can you recall seeing family members making lists and receiving and sending mail?
10. Did you receive and send mail (such as birthday cards, thank-you notes, letters) when you were a child?
11. Can you remember any other indications that reading and writing were valued in the environment in which you grew up?
12. Can you detail your first memories of reading and writing instruction? Materials used? Methods of teaching? Content?
13. Can you recall reading for pleasure in elementary school?
14. Can you remember writing for pleasure in elementary school?
15. Can you recall the first book you chose to read in elementary school?
16. Can you recall your first writing assignment in elementary school?
17. Did you write a report in elementary school?
18. Do you remember the purposes for your reading and writing in elementary school? Do you recall any particular type of instruction you received? Can you describe any instructional materials that were used?
19. Did you have a library card when you were in elementary school? Did you use it then? In later school years?
20. Can you recall the first book you loved (couldn't put down)?

(continued)

FIGURE 1   Literacy History Prompts *(continued)*

21. Do you feel that you've ever read a book that has made a difference in your life?
22. Have you ever read a book that you knew had been challenged or censored? How did you feel about reading it?
23. Were you a reader in your intermediate and/or junior high school years?
24. Can you pleasurably recall sharing books with friends?
25. Did you read a certain type of book (such as mysteries or biographies) at a particular age? Why do you think you made such choices?
26. When did you first visit a book store? What was it like?
27. Were you required to read certain novels in junior high or high school? How did you feel about that?
28. What is your all-time favorite children's book? Novel? Nonfiction work?
29. Have you ever seen a book you've read turned into a film?
30. Have there been times in your life when you have viewed reading as a pleasurable activity?
31. Have there been times in your life when you have viewed writing as a pleasurable activity?
32. What contributions have your reading and writing abilities made to your life?
33. Are you a reader now?
34. Are you a writer now?
35. Do you feel comfortable modeling reading and writing for your students?
36. What are you currently reading? Writing?

(McLaughlin, 1994)

STUDENTS' LITERACY HISTORIES

The availability of the prompts has not appeared to restrict our students' freedom in recounting their experiences. Each literacy history has emerged as a unique record of a particular individual's development. This is demonstrated in the following examples of students' literacy histories. Debbie Wallitsch, a student in the young adult literature course, is the author of the first work.

My Literacy History

When I was very young, I used to love saying poetry with my mother. I had no idea at the time what I was doing. I only knew I was acting like my mother and having a great time. My very earliest recollections of writing samples are at age two and a half.

When I phoned my mom tonight, I asked her if I was crazy or if I really scribbled (writing to a two-year-old) in her cookbooks and on her recipe cards. I could not imagine being able to remember this at only two and a half years old. She asked me if I wanted her to mail me a copy of the writing samples to be evaluated. I told her that wouldn't be necessary.

I remember being read to all the time as a child. My fondest memories are of my mother and me in the burnt orange puffy chair reading stories. She would read to me and I would follow along looking at the pictures. She claims to have read to me when I was in the womb. At age two, my favorite book which I never put down was the *S&H Green Stamp Book*. I would chase my mother around the house carrying this book every waking hour of my day. When we finally sat down to read it, she would begin by asking, "Where's the lamp?" and it was my job to find the lamp and all the other objects. We would do this for hours at a time.

I also remember at age three to pretend to read books. My neighbor who was six at the time would always come over to our house with her school books and I would read them with her. Sometimes I would sit in the reading chair and babble through my own books, making them up as I went along. I believe the first book I ever read was at age three. *Snow* and *Go, Dog, Go* by Dr. Seuss were the first books I read from memory. I also remember reading a Richard Scarry book with numerous pages of illustrations in it. I would name each of the items on the page. I specifically remember the page with the house on it. I could name the items in each of the rooms. I don't remember ever reading from the book *Green Eggs and Ham* but I remember reciting it in the bathtub on occasion as a very young girl.

My father was a high school English teacher and had an entire library of books at home. I can barely remember a time when my dad didn't have a book in his hand. He was also a sports fanatic and subscribed to many sports magazines along with *Reader's Digest*, *Time*, among others. I also received *Jack and Jill* as a young child. Magazines I remember from my later years are *World* by National Geographic Society and *Swimming World*. My parents belonged to a book club and purchased books on a monthly basis. These, as well as all of our magazines, were organized in our den on shelves.

I was always encouraged to read and write. I can remember my mom helping me with letters to my grandmother. She would write the letters and I would copy them on to a card. I would send thank you notes to friends and relatives when appropriate. I am positive that reading and writing were extremely valued in the environment in which I grew up. As a child, I never knew how much of an asset this was for my future schooling.

I was reading when I went to kindergarten at age five. I was placed in a first grade reading class, and bumped up the next year to second grade reading as well. I don't remember why, I just remember loving to read. I remember my mother taking me out of Miss Sherwood's phonetic reading class and placing me in Mrs. DeWan's holistic class. The first writing activities I remember in school were using fat pencils on wide-ruled paper copying letters in no particular order. Basically, handwriting lessons to me were writing.

Surprisingly, I remember reading for pleasure in the early years. Not only do I remember reading, I remember my favorite places in the classroom to do my silent reading. I think it's because I am currently teaching in the district where I went to school and have had my memory refreshed by frequenting these classrooms while conversing with my colleagues. However, something must have been positive for me to remember it. I especially recall reading in the wooden rocking boat in kindergarten and first grade. I never placed any importance on this until I realized that my favorite place to read at home is my porch swing. I wonder if there's any correlation?

I do not remember writing for pleasure in any grade up until eighth grade. The only story I ever recall writing in school was recently given to me by my fifth-grade teacher upon her retirement. As soon as I saw the cover, I remembered the specific activity. The first book I ever remember reading from the school library was *Mike Mulligan and the Steam Shovel*. I'm sure I checked out many books at the public library prior to this as my mom and I made weekly trips to the library. I can remember always leaving school with the maximum number of library books you were allowed to have and wanting to exchange them a few days later prior to our classroom book exchange time.

My clearest recollections of reading and writing instruction are from a basal reader, as well as SRAs. I never remember being taught how to write, only handwriting. My reading memories are a little clearer because I was accelerated into a different grade in the early years. In third grade I recall the only different scenario. Mrs. Foster, who greatly influenced me to become a teacher, taught us reading by not only using the basal but with literature books. She read *Charlie and the Chocolate Factory* and *Mrs. Frisby and the Rats of NIMH* to us as well as many others. Her enthusiasm while reading is an image I always keep in mind as I read aloud to my students. It was in third grade that I remember developing a true love of reading. The book I never wanted to put down was *Charlotte's Web*. Many times people would come to me to get the book because I always had the library's copy.

The years from third to eighth grade were most unpleasant to me. I do not recall ever writing with the exception of my fifth-grade story previously mentioned and a seventh- grade English assignment which I still have somewhere in my closet. Mrs. Ryan integrated a consumer unit into our grammar lessons. I remember I wrote a letter to Pert shampoo commenting on their product. I'll never forget the day I received a letter back from the President of Pert which included a free sample. We also created our own products and evaluated the different types of advertising used by companies. We created our own advertisements through whatever medium we chose for our original products. I'll never forget the 98% I received on that project. It was the best grade I earned in seventh grade.

I recall reading class being boring. Even though I excelled in the primary years, my grades dropped considerably due to my lack of interest. All I wanted to do was read my books and not be bothered by workbook pages. I also went through a troubling time with an addiction from which my father suffered. I escaped through books. This is when I remember reading different kinds of literature. It was not until my eighth-grade reading class that I began to value reading as a process. Mr. Joyce was the first reading teacher since Mrs. Foster in third grade who realized my love for books, not for the basal or SRA's. It was in his class I remember doing other activities like writing short stories, including all five story elements. Mr. Joyce made me feel like my stories were worthwhile and valuable. We also explored poetry of different types. We did research and reports on famous people of our choice. Even though I did some of this work in Mr. Joyce's lunch detention, I loved it all the same. As a matter of fact, I think I liked lunch detention with Mr. Joyce because we often talked about different books we had read.

During my high school years I became very involved in athletics and my pleasure reading declined. I read what I needed to read for school and that was it. I didn't like the books that made me think about what I was reading. I would rather have read for pure enjoyment. During the summer of my sophomore year, we were assigned to read ten novels of our choice from a master list. Our assignment was to summarize these stories and react to them. I remember my favorites as *The Catcher in the Rye*, *Summer of My German Soldier*, and *Of Mice and Men*. Other than that summer, I do not remember reading for pleasure unless it was from a magazine like *Teen* or *Young Miss*. It was usually magazine articles I remember sharing with my friends.

Just the fact that I was so exposed to reading and writing as a young child, I think, has influenced me more than any one book. If I had to choose the one book that changed my life, it would be very hard. Books in general changed my life by providing me with an outlet during a very difficult time of my adolescent years. My all-time favorite children's book that I still read every year is *James and the Giant Peach*. *For Whom the Bell Tolls* ranks up there among my favorite novels but many are close.

Through college, I loved to read for pleasure. Many of the books I read were made into movies. After I viewed the movie, I liked to go back and read the book again to better compare the two. I have always viewed reading as a pleasurable activity. I only wish I could say the same about writing. I enjoy writing letters and narratives but that is where my enjoyment ends. After completing this literacy history, I am wondering if there is any correlation between my lack of interest in writing and the lack of creative writing I did during my school years? After starting my master's program, I have found my interest in writing increasing, especially if I am interested in what I am writing about. The classes I have chosen are of interest to me and I learn from what I am writing about, therefore, my writing is worthwhile and valuable.

There is no doubt in my mind that my love for reading has made me a more well-rounded person, as well as a better teacher. I feel that I will always love reading for two reasons. First, pleasurable reading is a great stress-reliever for me. It has always been a way for me to relax and lose myself and all my problems for a little while. Second, in the profession which I have chosen, I need to continually read to make my teaching better. I enjoy reading teaching magazines, as well as psychology, administrative, and other journals to keep on top of educational issues.

At this point in my life I consider myself a writer. I have also adapted writing into my stress reduction plan by writing feelings down when angry or confused. I need to see things written out in order to make sound decisions. I try to convey to my students my writing mishaps in the past, and how my feelings about writing have changed over the years. When my students do a creative writing assignment, I do it at the same time they do it. Not only does it help me enhance my writing skills, it allows my students to see that I feel writing is worthwhile activity.

I am currently reading a Mary Higgins Clark novel in my free time. I constantly read a variety of magazines. My husband and I subscribe to too many to list. Most of my reading during the past four weeks as well as the next five will be from professional journals which will tie into my current writings which are directly related to my summer session courses.

This literacy history has brought back many pleasant memories of reading. While the memories of writing are not quite as treasured, they certainly explain some of my feelings about the writing process. This was very helpful in that I have become more aware of what I need to better model for my students. I also have some new stories to pass on to them about my reading and writing that were stimulated by this literacy project. This literacy history was definitely a pleasurable writing experience.

When writing their literacy histories, some students choose to write narrative accounts of their literacy development, and others select alternative formats. These include poems, audiotapes, videotapes, timelines, and various other artistic interpretations. Claire Hansen, a student in the secondary reading methods class, wrote this poem about her life in sixth grade, as part of her literacy history.

Reading Group

Words that jump all over the page,
Never standing still, always different, never the same,
How can I control them, make them listen to me?

Concentrate, meditate, force them to behave,
Please won't you listen? I know I'll have to pay,
If I can't control you, she will strike again.

The teacher's coming to my group to listen to me read,
I'll tell her I don't feel well and ask if I can leave.
I will just say, "No thank you, I don't care to read."
But she insists and so I start...fear mounts inside of me.

I begin on the first line, but nothing's making sense,
Only jumbled words pop out and then I feel the blow,
Her hand is slapping mine and then her angry voice.

"No, that's not right. It makes no sense.
You'll have to start again."
I feel the blow upon my hand and I begin again.

This goes on until she stops, frustrated only with me,
"Oh! Stop this nonsense reading,"
She says, "I guess you just can't read!"

Creating literacy histories promotes reflectivity. Personal, distinctive accounts of each individual's experiences emerge with the literacy process. In addition, the insights gained from preservice teachers' literacy histories offer an authentic commentary on educational practices from the participants' perspective (McLaughlin, 1994). Additional examples of students' literacy histories can be found in Chapter 5 and Appendix D.

REFLECTIVITY THROUGHOUT THE PORTFOLIO PROCESS

After students create their literacy histories, they extend their reflectivity to conferences, small-group discussion, rationale statements, and self-assessment of portfolios. Each of these aspects of portfolio assessment offers students opportunities to "walk inside their own heads."

CONFERENCES

Portfolio conferences are inquiry based. Meaningful questions are asked by students and professors. Both also engage in reflection to support and clarify their thinking. During conferences the students' performances are either affirmed or revised. (Chapter 6 offers more details about conferences.)

SMALL-GROUP DISCUSSION

Small-group portfolio discussions contribute to a sense of community and generally reduce anxiety. They build confidence and offer direction to particular performances or the portfolio in general. Reflection during these discussions is often more expansive as students contemplate not only their own portfolios but also their peers'.

RATIONALE STATEMENTS

The value of student reflectivity may be demonstrated most clearly in the students' rationale statements. These establish a sense of conviction about personal choices. They delineate each learning goal's meaning and make connections between the goal and the students' performances. Further, rationale statements document individual growth and validate the authenticity of the portfolio process. Examples of student rationale statements can be found in Chapter 5 and Appendix D.

PORTFOLIO SELF- AND PEER EVALUATION

Prior to submitting their portfolios, students engage in self-evaluation. This requires them to reflect on how well they have progressed toward attaining each course goal. Self-evaluation entails using the portfolio rubric and offering a rationale for the suggested evaluation. Further, students often engage in similar individual or group processes when evaluating peer portfolios. (See Chapter 6 for a complete discussion of evaluation.)

A FINAL THOUGHT

Through their reflections, students come to view learning as a process, realize what they know and what they do not, make connections to other courses, and learn that their thinking is valued and respected. This leads to new questions and continued self-reflection. As Brandt (1991, p. 3) has noted, "Thinking about what we are doing leads us to ask better questions, break out of fruitless routines, make unexpected connections, and experiment with fresh ideas."

The information students so openly share in the reflective aspects of the portfolio process directly supports the portfolio's "advantage of encouraging self-reflection and examination of growth over time, aspects of learning rarely captured in standardized tests or even in the newer once-a-year performance tasks" (Valencia, Hiebert, & Afflerbach, 1994, p. 290). In our experience with situated assessment, these reflective experiences have emerged as authentic contributors not only to students' ownership of the assessment process, but also to ownership of their literacy.

CHAPTER FIVE

The portfolio allowed me to express myself in my own way. It made me realize things I knew that I didn't even know I knew. It made me think and get to know myself better as a person and as a learner. Self-discovery is what this portfolio has been about for me. It shows who I am.

Alexandra Weldon
This passage by Weldon, a student in the elementary reading methods class, is excerpted from a reflection on the role of assessment in the instructional process.

VENTURING INSIDE STUDENT PORTFOLIOS

THIS CHAPTER REPRESENTS the culmination of the portfolio process. It shows the choices our students made, the performances they created, and the reflectivity in which they engaged as their learning evolved. The student work presented in this chapter reflects the diversity found within each portfolio. These individual pieces have been submitted as partial evidence of students' understanding and application of the respective goals. Although each of these selections demonstrates synthesis of learning, it is important to emphasize that each student submits multiple, self-selected indicators to document achievement of each course goal. Additional examples of student performances can be found in Appendix D.

ELEMENTARY READING METHODS COURSE EXAMPLES

As mentioned in Chapter 2, one of the goals for the elementary reading methods course is

> By the end of the course of study, students will be able to demonstrate knowledge and application of curriculum, instruction, and assessment.

In her reflection on this goal, Carmen Orner wrote about the importance of creating strategic readers and supported her thoughts with evidence including a thematic plan and a lesson plan. What follows is her rationale statement. It documents what she discovered about cooperative learning and the value of peer interaction, student reactions, and teaching experience.

> By teaching my students early in their elementary years to be strategic readers, I know they will be prepared to understand and learn while they are reading. I feel strongly about developing students' reading skills and habits of reading early. When the work gets increasingly harder each year, they will already have the experience and practice of strategic reading and they won't have to

worry because their reading foundation has already been established. Two of the evidences I have included to support this goal are my thematic unit and a lesson plan.

Evidence One, a thematic unit, was created with my peers. My group chose to explore multiculturalism. Our plan introduces our topic, shares our goals, presents appropriate lessons including assessment and evaluation practices, and includes a culminating activity and annotated list of print, audio, and visual resources.

One of the ways that thematic instruction benefits the students is by incorporating several different academic areas. In our unit we have developed lessons for reading/language arts, social studies, science, art, and music to expose the children to a variety of different experiences and lessons that promote literacy learning as an active, constructive process. This will also help the children to develop in-depth knowledge about multiculturalism. By participating in the thematic plan students will also be able to learn that their ability to use strategies extends across the curriculum.

I learned a lot about multiculturalism from this experience, but I also learned a lot about working in a group. I think this is important because when I have my own classroom, I will need to work as part of the faculty team.

My second evidence is a lesson plan about the book *Moe the Dog in Tropical Paradise*. I developed it to include the use of skills and strategies before, during, and after reading. I activated prior knowledge to help motivate the students and created a writing activity to extend their learning. I really enjoyed actually teaching this lesson when we visited our partner elementary school. I've included a narrative about that experience because I think it's important to share what it was like to teach the lesson and how the children reacted.

It was really rewarding to see this plan in action. The children had so many different perspectives to share. Their background experiences and ideas for writing a sequel really showed the diversity of their thinking. I learned that it is one thing to create a lesson plan, but it's quite another to be part of bringing the plan to life.

Another student, Eve Slater, submitted her experience as a volunteer at the Reading Department's annual Young Authors' Day as supporting evidence for the learning goal of demonstrating knowledge and application of curriculum, instruction, and assessment. After the author, Jerry Palotta, spoke, Eve and other volunteer education majors facilitated writing projects involving small groups of students. Eve submitted her reflection on this experience and the story the children wrote as partial evidence to support this goal. The following reflection records what Eve learned about cooperative learning and diversity of student thought.

This was a wonderful experience. Mr. Palotta is an entertaining speaker as well as writer. I was not familiar with his alphabet books and was delighted to see such innovative and different themes.

When we broke off into our groups to write stories, I was reminded of the diversity of writing styles and themes that young authors can implement. There was a boy who clearly had a descriptive and sensitive air to ideas. He wanted to create a picture of a lovely scene in the mind of the reader. One girl was determined to make it a silly story. She wanted humor included. Another girl wanted a mystery. And there was a group of children who clearly felt uncomfortable with the risk of sharing their ideas in the group. I tried to encourage them to contribute. Some did, but others just seemed too shy.

Conversely, there was one girl who really just wanted to write the story herself. Rather than confining herself to contributing one sentence or idea as the other children had, she tried to monopolize the rest of the story when it was her turn. She was very imaginative and suggested lots of different plots and twists for the story. She told us she thought our story was boring. The problem was that her idea of excitement reminded me of bad television. She wanted a "good" disaster theme. First she wanted the mother and father in the story to be divorced because the father was a drunk (her words) and beat the family. She wanted the mall in the story to collapse and kill us all. The group finally included her idea of Santa stealing toys by compromising that it had only occurred in a dream.

Working with a group of students to produce one story was a really interesting experience. It was a challenge to include the diverse ideas that were put forth, but we all really had fun writing it. This was a true cooperative learning experience. Watching the children negotiate with each other concerning which ideas would appear in the story was fascinating. Compromise was clearly the path to success. I think publishing these group stories is a great idea because it shows the students that we value what they wrote and provides them with a memory of their experiences with children from other schools and their time with the author.

Another goal for the elementary reading methods course is

> By the end of the course of study, students will be able to demonstrate knowledge and application of authentic literature and its role in the instructional process.

The following is the text of a children's book created by two students. In their rationale statements for the learning goal, the authors, Alison Hughes and Rebecca Urritia, each spoke about the value of authentic literature as the basis of instruction and how their story of a unique student was inspired by their hopes of becoming special education teachers. In addition to the book itself, each student submitted lesson plans incorporating skills and strategies such as predicting, story mapping, and engaging in creative writing. In reflecting on the book and her lesson, Alison noted that creating the book was especially interesting because it allowed her to experience what her students will experience when they write stories. She also felt that being an author would better prepare her to model for her students. Rebecca remarked that it would be very important to her that her students see her as a reader and a writer. She also felt that it was a good idea to be able to show students that their skills and strategies can be applied to any story. Both Alison and Rebecca concluded their rationale statements by describing how the story was used in their field experience teaching. The children in the class responded enthusiastically, many identifying with being the new person in a particular situation. The students were also excited to learn that their teachers were the authors of the text. Here is the story:

The Star

Mrs. Oval stood in front of the class and greeted her pupils, "Welcome to Shapeville Elementary. I'm very excited to get to know all of you. As you know, this is a very special school for shapes like you and me. This school is special because we learn when all the humans are fast asleep and it is very dark outside!" Mrs. Oval pointed out the window, smiled at her students, and continued with her happy hello. "The word *special* is my favorite of all words, and we are going to be learning about the word special. I have a little story to tell you about being special. Did any of you ever wonder where the first star came from?"

The children nodded their heads and mumbled a very shy, "Yes."

"Okay then, I'll tell you."

Mrs. Oval began to tell her story. "About ten years ago I taught a group of first-grade shapes and there was a star shape in my class. I can remember her first day during recess..."

"May I play jump rope with you?"

The children giggled and whispered to each other. One of the young shapes who was known for being a bully piped up and asked, "Who are *you*?"

The star replied softly, "My name is Sabrina and I'm new to Shapeville. What's your name?"

The bold triangle answered, "My name is TRACEY!"

Sabrina asked again if she could play with the children. Cindy the circle said, "Come on, let her play!"

Before Cindy could finish her sentence, Tracey the triangle said, "No! She might cut the ropes with those points on her! What kind of shape is she anyway?"

"Sabrina sunk her head and walked away, and I was the only one who heard her say quietly that she was a star..." said Mrs. Oval to her class.

Mrs. Oval continued to tell her story. "I sat at my desk and watched for months as Sabrina was left out of the games. It wasn't until after one of my lessons that my class learned how very special and unique Sabrina was."

I remember clearly that we were discussing how each of us was very unique. "Now each and every one of you is so very important and special. You all have the ability to do whatever you want when you grow up. You all can make a big difference in this world. Would anyone like to share what they want to be when they grow up?"

Tracey the triangle was the first to reply, "I want to be a slice of pizza, because *everyone* likes pizza!"

Stephen the square said he wanted to be a beautiful mosaic tile, while Raoul the rectangle said he wanted to be a great big skyscraper. Sweet Cindy the circle said she wanted to be a bright green wagon wheel.

I turned to Sabrina and waited a little bit before I asked, "And what would you like to be?" She had no reply. She just sat there and cried because she did not know. She carried on for what seemed to be forever because the children just stared at her. What was even worse was that Tracey the triangle laughed at her tears.

Sabrina was so upset, she ran out of the classroom. The students and I watched from the window as Sabrina made her way down to the playground. We noticed that her dull colors began to wash off with the falling of her tears. Then we witnessed a spectacular sight. All of Sabrina's colors faded away; they were all gone!! Her colors were so brilliant that they pushed her up into the night sky. Her beams of light shined and shimmered. The rays were so powerful that they reached down to the school house and even hit the lonely jump rope lying on the playground. Sabrina found out that night how SPECIAL she really was. Sabrina still shines in the sky tonight, and sometimes I even catch her winking at the other young stars of Shapeville Elementary.

SECONDARY READING METHODS COURSE EXAMPLES

The first goal for the secondary reading methods course is

By the end of the course of study, students will be able to demonstrate knowledge and application of the history of elementary and secondary literacy instruction and the relation between that history and their own literacy development.

Students reflect on their own literacy histories while making connections with the history and trends of literacy instruction in the United States to accommodate this goal. The following poem connects the student's own literacy background with the historical trends in a comprehensive and thoughtful way. The poem briefly mentions the origins of tracking, grouping students according to their ability, and then relates the author's personal experiences with the practice. It is excerpted from a lengthier work which integrated both poetry and narrative. In the rationale statement preceding the learning goal, the author, Mick Wager, reflected, "To write a poem about a subject, one must be immersed in that subject." Displaying his understanding in this format enabled him to integrate his memories while advocating more humane ways of teaching.

Tracks were laid
the first half of the century
when teaching kids efficiently
involved proceeding on rails like products from a factory...

I know a bright guy who was stuck
in a class that did not match
his intelligence and was
not challenged
was not interested
did not excel

but did
enough
to pass
like a stone
gathering no moss.

I know I slipped onto a track
that went a little fast
for me, but was pulled
along by the current.
I kept my head
above the water
better for the fight.

...a track that's not your own
can lead to a place

not your own
invention or desire.
Nothing is so steel-fire
cast like the future
of a child misdirected.

The artwork on the following pages shows other examples of students' literacy histories. Kyle Fukumoto took another approach by creating a cartoon that also decries tracking. Although his own literacy history details what he believes to be key elements in his development, the timeline he created is a bit sparse. Still, the overall effect is interesting and creative, and the performance clearly demonstrates Kyle's level of understanding and application. His drawing is on pages 53–54.

Another course goal for the secondary methods course is

By the end of the course of study, students will be able to demonstrate knowledge and application of the interrelation between assessment and instruction in secondary content areas.

For this goal, Brian Caulfield compared his perceptions of what it was like to be a student in classes where teachers just told students to "read the chapter and answer the questions" to his thoughts on current methods of teaching that include a variety of instructional strategies. From the class text and student discussion, he had learned alternatives to the more traditional lecture model, and he cleverly titled books with the names of the strategies he considered to be effective. He created the cartoon on page 55 to demonstrate his understandings, and in his detailed rationale statement he explained each of the techniques pictured on the book jackets. He then gave brief examples of how these strategies could be used in a history classroom.

Allen Harrison, a student in the secondary reading methods class, also used drawings to explain his understandings of scaffolded instruction for less experienced readers and second language learners. On pages 56–58 he demonstrates how a teacher can provide scaffolding through appropriate modeling. In his rationale statement, Allen explained how a teacher can scaffold instruction in drawing by taking a student through the process one step at a time.

Kyle's Drawing

I WAS A VICTIM OF TRACKING!

(FICTIONALIZED but TRUE) by Kyle F.

Me → Cerebrus

My scholastic career began at Primanti Montessori preschool in Anaheim. I remember where it was because I was expecting to go to Disneyland. My dad remembers that they taught us the names of dinosaurs...

Now what is this? / Tyranno-saurus rex Mouse

What I remember from those days was jigsaw puzzles and a field trip to a dairy. My mom says that the school was innovative in that it treated the "child as an individual person."

Vacuum / Pasteurized milk / Moo

My mom wanted me to have a regular curriculum though. I hated to go to school so my mom introduced me to the real world by pushing me out of the car. She enrolled me at Wittmann Elementary School down the street.

I started reading at about the 2nd grade. I think my first book was either Goodnight Moon or Green Eggs & Ham. My favorite game was playing "Greek Myths" from out of Bulfinch's Mythology.

Hit record? THE WAILERS / WITTMANN PRESENT

My favorite book in elementary school was The Incredible Journey. We sang songs and even made a Christmas album as the Wittmann Wailers. We wrote and drew stories from what we could remember learning how to draw, tell from the cover of a book.

Death Star / "TIE" fighter

My mom says that phonics teaching was started in the district when I arrived. She says that the teachers weren't trained to teach [it]. I don't remember learning phonics, but I do remember learning how to draw,

Are you my teacher or a dinosaur? / Moo!

Other teaching strategies were tried in class. Team teaching involved moving students from class to class, but it was too confusing." The "open classroom" allowed students to move around, but the "noise level was too high."

(continued)

Kyle's Drawing (continued)

my first somewhat light & easy poem & moon were the blue & white ... The shining city of real and ... These were lined in the ... streaking by. The city ...

In December 1981, I was enrolled in a creative writing class at Cerritos College. Our instructor printed our writing in a booklet at the end of the class. Later, in high school I submitted short stories for contests.

What just happened here?

Faye Ross Junior High is a blur in my memory. I was not a motivated student and was given basic classes until my Sophomore year of high school. Tracking had taken another victim.

▲ My old pal Adam + a tracking epiphany

At Gahr High School, I did well in my English classes and got into college prep. I ran into a friend from my basic classes and asked him, "Why are you still in the stupid classes?" He replied happily, "I like being dumb!"

I played catch-up with my classes. My finest distinction was reading *Les Miserables* for a book report. My Junior English teacher uses me today as an example of a good reader. In Senior English, we wrote in journals.

☆ U.S. ☆ Literacy Instruction Timeline

So, where do I fit in here?

1600's Reading instruction was developmental.

1930's Research into learning problems.

1940's Remedial reading programs established

1950's Launching of Sputnik launches improved instruction.

1960's Strict federal guidelines cause staff problems with reading programs.

(Here I Am!)

1970's ESL & special education programs phonics

Reading programs in most schools.

1980's "Reading Across the Curriculum"

1990's Expanded reading & writing instruction.

THE END

"Every teacher a Teacher of Reading"

Brian's Drawing

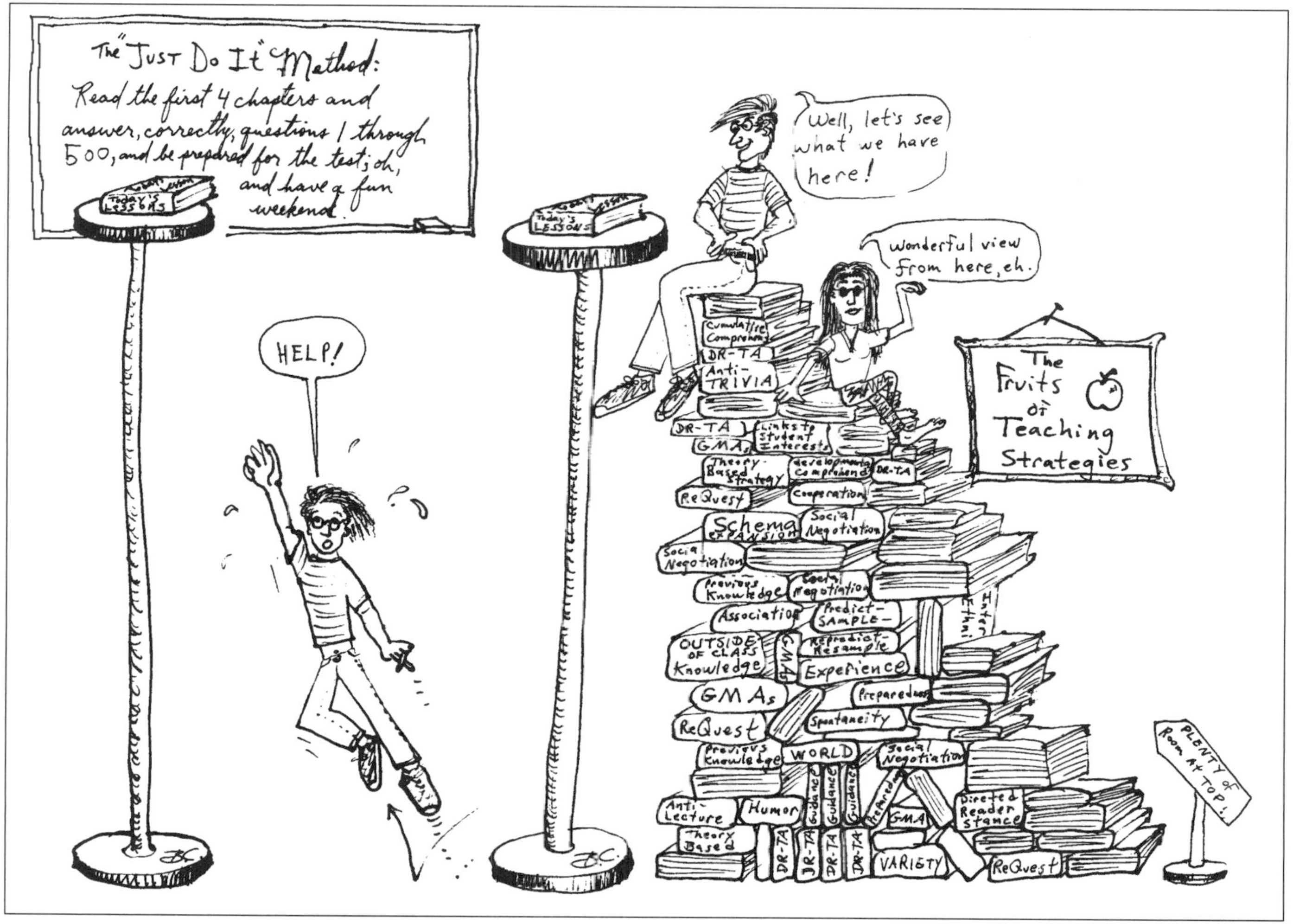

A RHINO

I am having problems drawing rhinos. I'm not artistically challenged, I can draw stick men (🧍). I just can't draw rhinos. I need extra help. I can do it myself. I just need a little extra instruction.

Fortunately, my teacher knows just what I need. I don't need any watered-down version of a rhino (like a stick-rhino). I want to draw the real thing. My teacher showed me how to draw a rhino, by drawing one. She/he is the perfect model. I watched my instructor's technique, but it seemed so foreign. I just couldn't grasp the concept so quickly. So...

(continued)

We continued to draw. I worked on the proportions so I could get a better overall idea of how to draw a rhino. My instructor was giving me the perfect scaffolds.

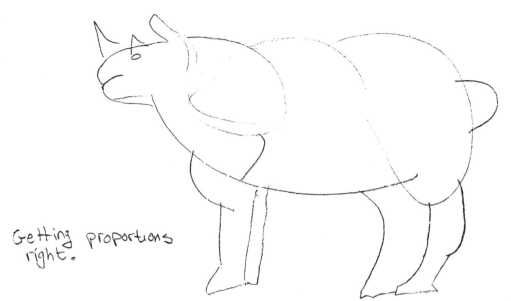

Getting proportions right.

In this drawing my instructor started the drawing for me. This is the closest thing I have to a rhino yet. But I won't quit, until I can do it myself.

Teacher Draws Head.

I draw body.

(continued)

Hey! I did it. I drew a terrific looking rhino. Boy is my instructor proud of me. But more importantly I'm proud of myself. There is no watered-down version of a rhino for me. Yet still I'm not quite happy with this...

A RHINO ↗

Now here's a rhino! My previous drawing was only a duplication of my instructor's rhino. True learning takes place when we follow our own path— my path led me to this rhino. Thanks to my instructor's careful planning, scaffolding, observations, and assessment (not to mention my hard work), my rhino is done. Next step is a pelican!

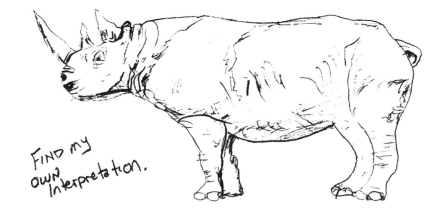

FIND MY OWN interpretation.

A Final Thought

Although the examples from students' portfolios featured in this chapter are typical of the types of material students submit, each of the examples was accompanied by other indicators and none of them was the sole piece of evidence submitted for a particular course learning goal. The total submission for each goal gives a clearer picture of the students' learning.

We have offered an array of student performances, but it is important to remember that there is no standard evidence to show understanding and application of a learning goal. The portfolios are as diverse as the students themselves. Each semester brings new surprises—humorous, creative, thoughtful representations of individual learners. We also should note that although we have shared print submissions in this chapter, pieces of evidence for learning goals are also commonly recorded on software, audio- and videotape, and other media.

CHAPTER SIX

I was excited to learn that we were going to be using portfolio assessment in this course. I had never created a portfolio before and I felt motivated to challenge myself. I wanted this portfolio to be the best possible example of my thinking, so I could reflect upon it and learn about myself. When I read what I've created, I can't help thinking, WOW! Did that really come from my head? I feel as if the whole learning process is brand new to me.

Laura Eilenberger
*This passage by Eilenberger, a student
in the elementary reading methods class,
is excerpted from a self-assessment
of the portfolio process.*

CONFERENCES AND EVALUATION

A FTER ALL THE planning, work, and discussion, it is time for the portfolios to be submitted. Class begins with small-group sharing of the portfolios and they are passed around, read, and received with displays of interest and enthusiasm. This time of sharing is very important because students have an opportunity to see what others have submitted, which helps them with their own self-assessment.

To get to this point, however, takes some work. This chapter discusses the issue of evaluating, from early student-teacher conferences to the final grade. Implicit in our use of portfolios is the assumption that each student's work is highly personalized and idiosyncratic. Portfolios differ according to presentation, style, content, and depth. Because of these inherent differences, the involved, intricate process of evaluation can be challenging.

CONFERENCES

Holding conferences serves a central role in the portfolio assessment process because it allows the professor to learn things about students that are not included in the portfolio itself (Desai, 1993; McLaughlin & Kennedy, 1992). Both the conference *and* the portfolio are needed to clearly understand students' thinking processes. Student-professor conferences are one of the great, unexpected benefits of portfolio assessment, and the dialogues that have emerged in these conferences are essential, valued components of our teaching.

The obvious challenge with conferences is time. Depending on the number of students enrolled in a course, holding individual conferences can take many hours. Students in the elementary methods courses have midterm and end of term conferences in addition to informal conferences throughout the semester. The secondary class has in-class conferences in addition to the professor's scheduled office hours for drop-in discussions. The purpose of these meetings, individual or small group, is for students to explain parts of their portfolios, discuss questions or issues, and receive feedback and support.

PORTFOLIO PLANNERS

Portfolio Planners represent an important step in the evaluation process. Two to three weeks before the portfolios are due, both at midterm and end of term, students use the Planners to describe the evidence they are submitting for each goal and how the evidence demonstrates their learning and application. The Planners help clarify expectations for what constitutes an appropriate submission. Figures 2 and 3 are examples of the Planners we use in our ele-

FIGURE 2   Portfolio Planner: Teaching of Reading in the Elementary School

This Portfolio Planner serves two purposes: first, it will help you organize your performances and reasoning as an initial step in creating your portfolio; second, it will serve as the basis for our planning conference.

Please write the goal you are addressing in the space provided. Then list each evidence that you plan to include to support your progress toward attaining the goal. After you have done that, revisit each evidence and explain how it relates to the goal.

Goal:

_____

_____

Evidences:

1._____

    Relationship to goal _____

_____

2._____

    Relationship to goal _____

_____

3._____

    Relationship to goal _____

_____

_____

Figure 3   Portfolio Planner: Teaching of Reading in the Secondary School

---

Name: _____ Class: Mon. Tues. Wed.

Goal 1: *Historical Trends*

a. Evidence(s) of personal literacy history:

b. Evidence(s) of knowledge of the history of literacy instruction:

c. Relation of evidence(s) to goal and connections between "a" and "b":

Goal 2: *Current Literacy Theories*

a. Evidence(s) of theoretical understandings:

b. Evidence(s) of application of theories to instruction:

c. Relation of evidence(s) to goal:

---

mentary and secondary reading methods courses. We have found that the more detail students include in the Planner, the more likely they are to be successful with their final portfolios. During conferences, the Planners serve as the focus for discussion; after conferences, they are a resource for making any student-initiated changes before the portfolio due date.

PORTFOLIO SHARING AND EVALUATION

On the portfolio due dates, when the portfolios are shared in small groups, students engage in self- and peer reflection. Later, time is spent debriefing about the portfolio experience. Students discuss their feelings about the process, the time they spent on their portfolios, and the depth and breadth of their learning. We encourage a frank discussion about the differences in preparation time for portfolios, traditional projects, and tests, as well as any concerns about grades.

Some students feel that the portfolio evaluation is almost secondary to the process of planning, gathering evidence, and writing rationale statements. However, the portfolios still clearly represent a course grade for the majority of students. Although assigning grades may seem antithetical to the portfolio process, most university policies require that professors accommodate a traditional grading system. Classroom teachers must also adhere to district grading policies. Therefore, by necessity, the role of the professor and teacher changes from coach to evaluator, and students may find this change frustrating.

However, when students engage in self-assessment and peers become part of the evaluation procedure, the redefined role of the professor as evaluator is not as problematic. A rubric that is collaboratively developed during class is completed by students and submitted along with their portfolios. Peers also review the portfolios during the sharing period and provide concrete and supportive feedback. This mirrors what is occurring with portfolios in many elementary and secondary schools. Ford (1994) handles the grading issue by having his graduate students write a detailed rationale for the grade they believe they deserve. This is followed by a conference and the professor's input. It is important to note that evaluation of the portfolios ultimately involves multiple views.

THE RUBRIC

When we first began evaluating portfolios, we wrote comments on the portfolio submissions and included a written summary sheet. However, in order to attain greater consistency in our evaluations, we decided to work with a rubric. A rubric is a scoring guide that offers a description of student performance, generally on a continuum. It is designed around the goals, expectations, or outcomes developed for the performance task (McLaughlin, 1995). This part of the assessment process is congruent with K–12 portfolio recommendations such as the New Standards Project, an association of states that has been developing learning standards and portfolio assessment procedures for elementary, middle, and high school students, and state assessment guidelines, such as those used by Arizona, Kentucky, Pennsylvania, and Maryland.

Each semester we begin with a skeletal rubric that has four levels: *exceptional*, *thorough*, *adequate*, and *inadequate*. We then complete a detailed rubric in class with our students. This step is very important to the process because the students gain understanding about how their portfolios will be evaluated and about the use of rubrics. We ask students in groups to determine what might constitute an *adequate* submission. This is difficult for the students to do at the beginning of the course because most of them are unfamiliar with the portfolio process. However, once we encourage them to think of their previous experiences in university courses, they are able to see that *adequate* has the same meaning, regardless of context. They then brainstorm descriptors for the other levels used in the rubrics: *exceptional*, *thorough*, and *inadequate*. These are shared with the entire class and together we determine a uniform meaning for each term. The detailed descriptors are then distributed to the class.

Because the students create the descriptors, they differ somewhat from semester to semester, yet they are remarkably similar and consistent. Examples of descriptors from one class follow:

- *Exceptional*: highly imaginative; demonstrates critical thought; unique; substantial application to own teaching; goes above and beyond requirements; creative; demonstrates both breadth and depth; shows individual's personality; professional in presentation and appearance; demonstrates considerable effort.

- *Thorough*: well organized and complete; effectively and clearly presented; demonstrates clear understandings; applies what has been learned to the classroom; clearly shows connections; detailed; thoughtful and supported with ideas.

- *Adequate*: meets minimum requirements; includes general information but lacks descriptive detail; some application to teaching; lacks originality.

- *Inadequate*: missing evidence or information; sloppy and poorly organized; demonstrates only surface understandings; no evidence of

65

application to teaching; poorly written or does not include rationale statement.

Other professors using portfolios report they also use evaluation rubrics but in a different manner. For example, P.D. Pearson (1994) uses a rubric with a 1 to 4 rating:

1 = awareness

2 = awareness + explanation

3 = awareness + explanation + application

4 = awareness + explanation + application + flexibility (the ability to adapt and modify)

Ford (1994) and his graduate students identify behaviors that constitute "A" level performance, such as "acquires knowledge inside and outside the classroom; applies what has been learned; shares knowledge with others; empowers and engages self; and displays a positive attitude toward learning" (p. 2). These descriptors were culled from an original list of 29 different behaviors identified by students during class.

It is important to note that students participate in rubric design in each of the examples just described. Most undergraduate and graduate students have had years of experience trying to determine what it takes to earn an "A" grade with *exceptional* work. Including students in the process of determining the meaning of the rubric designations has had a powerful effect in our courses. Apprehension about "how much evidence is enough" and "how good is good" have been greatly reduced, and students have taken more ownership of the evaluation process.

The final rubrics for our elementary and secondary reading methods courses are formatted with the indicators for each goal listed on the left. For each indicator, we can place an "X" on the corresponding descriptor for each goal. We then follow with substantive written comments. Our written responses are a critical factor in the evaluation. They document questions we had during reading the portfolio submissions, and we try to make them as detailed as possible. A sample portfolio evaluation for an elementary reading methods course, which details the use of the rubric and the emphasis on written comments, is shown in Figure 4. (Additional completed sample evaluation sheets using the rubric are in Appendix C.)

FIGURE 4   Portfolio Submission 1   Spring

Name: XXXXXXX

Goal 1: Knowledge and application of contemporary theories of literacy
　　　instruction.

	Exceptional	Thorough	Adequate	Inadequate
Indicator 1	X			
Indicator 2		X		
Indicator 3			X	
Overall submission		X		

Your rationale statements are insightful and clearly align your performances
with the goal. Your literacy history was wonderfully creative. You had quite an interesting emergence into literacy! Your series of interviews with the teacher was an
especially meaningful evidence. It showed both what you know from the questions
you asked and how the teacher instructs from a constructivist perspective. Your
discussion of the role of constructivism in the Lipson and Wixson interactive model and your application of it to the classroom examples of a strategic reader were
also very creative and effective.

As I noted in our conference, this is a marvelous start to your portfolio. You
have clearly achieved this goal.

___

Writing most of our comments on the computer and not on the portfolio
expedites the portfolio evaluation process. The fun part is watching the students
read our comments and register surprise that we have actually read every word
of their portfolios. We both have had students tell us they seldom receive such
extended personal reflections from their professors.

The last step in the evaluation process is to determine a grade for the
portfolio. Some professors choose to assign a letter grade for the entire portfolio as a composite piece; we rely on the rubric to guide our evaluation and

each course goal is scored holistically. One of us associates the rubric designation (*exceptional* to *inadequate*) with a letter grade (A to D). The other assigns points for each of the weighted goals; these are then totaled for a course grade at the end of the semester. (See Appendix B for course syllabi and additional information about grading practices.)

The most important thing we have learned about reading and evaluating portfolios is to allow ample time. Because they are individualistic and include material that is unique, personal, and creative, the submissions must be read thoroughly and carefully. In fact, it is the singular nature of the portfolios that makes them so enjoyable, satisfying, and frequently exciting to read.

RESUBMISSION POLICY

Occasionally students submit work that is poorly done. If a student receives the equivalent of *adequate* or *inadequate* for the midterm submission, we offer the chance to resubmit. Following a conference, a timeline is negotiated, suggestions for improvement are made, revisions are completed, and the portfolio is resubmitted. To ensure fairness to other students, we explain that the highest grade possible on a resubmission is the equivalent of a "B" or *thorough*. We have found that a resubmission policy lessens anxiety and allows another chance for those students who try hard but have initial difficulty with the process. We also should note that implementing the Portfolios Planners has reduced the number of students who resubmit.

GRADE DISTRIBUTIONS

Not surprisingly, at the beginning of the portfolio process we had some concerns about how our grades would be distributed. Though neither of us is bound by university distribution requirements (so many A's, B's, or C's), we wondered if our prior distributions would remain the same for portfolios. We have found that course grade distributions with portfolios are very similar to patterns established with traditional grading practices. While investigating grade distributions over a ten year period, Ruddell (Vogt, McLaughlin, & Ruddell, 1993) found that slightly more students earned an A grade using portfolios than with traditional grading, and fewer earned B grades. Grades in the C, D, and F range remained relatively constant. It has been suggested that this finding could be interpreted in support of the reliability of portfolio assessment;

that is, portfolio grade distributions are similar to traditional grade profiles. Or, it could be used to argue that portfolio assessment yields greater benefits for students because more earn A grades.

We, however, have attributed the positive differences—the slight increase in A grades—to: (1) students' heightened awareness of course outcomes and grading practices; (2) an evaluation based on multiple indicators; (3) students' freedom to select evidence to support course outcomes and focus on their own strengths; and (4) the provision for resubmission of midterm portfolios receiving an *adequate* or lower evaluation.

In all, the distribution of grades has not been a problem. There is a clear distinction between those portfolios that are *exceptional* and those that are *inadequate*. The differences between the *exceptional* (or A) portfolios and those that are *thorough* (or B) are not as clear, but with the detailed rubrics that are returned to students following each submission, we are able to explain how the *thorough* submissions differ from the *exceptional* ones. We have encountered no grade appeals or problems with the issuance of grades.

It appears that because students have greater ownership of the portfolio process than they did with traditional evaluation, they believe they actually *earn* the grades that are assigned. This sense of ownership often results in interesting confessions, such as, "I know this is the very best work I could have done," or "I know I could have done much better with this piece of evidence."

We have been asked by colleagues whether students ever finish the course with an inadequate evaluation equivalent to a failing grade. This may seem antithetical to authentic assessment, but the reality is that a student's failure to submit adequate evidence of his or her understandings and applications can happen. However, we usually are able to intervene and provide support early in the semester because of the intensive assessment process: introducing the concept in class; supporting small-group discussions about questions and concerns; using the Portfolio Planners; holding individual and group conferences; and encouraging student self-evaluations. This does not mean that a student who submits incomplete, careless, or late work will earn a passing grade; it just means that failing grades are rarely given.

RELIABILITY AND VALIDITY

Issues of reliability and validity are central to any discussion of grading practices. In order to ensure greater reliability, it is recommended that portfolios be "prepared to respond to a standard task or set of tasks" (Gellman, 1992–1993, p. 41). Portfolio assessment in our courses meets this criterion. Although the material submitted differs considerably from student to student, a common set of criteria guide preparation. Our course goals and portfolio possibilities contribute to uniformity and consistency. (See Chapter 3 for a discussion of goals and possibilities.)

Multiple indicators of student learning also contribute to reliability. Additionally, because our syllabi are detailed, students receive clear direction for their portfolio preparation. The Portfolio Planners, conferences, class discussions, sharing and collaboration, and evaluation sheets all are included to decrease student confusion and frustration. These procedures not only display sound pedagogy, but they also are serious attempts to ensure reliability.

The issue of reliability has been discussed at various professional meetings (Bruneau, 1995). Student portfolios from throughout the country have been shared and methods for evaluating them reviewed. As with holistic assessment practices in K–12 school settings, interrater reliability can be established through colleagues' reviewing and evaluating common pieces of evidence. In our collaboration, we have frequently shared student work in order to make certain our perceptions were accurate and consistent with our rubrics.

Ensuring validity in the portfolio process does not appear to be as problematic as ensuring reliability. Barton and Collins (1993) believe that portfolios represent a valid measure of student growth because they provide access to complex variables that contribute to students' overall learning and ability. Our system of evaluation measures what our students have learned and the degree to which they can apply that knowledge because it is "grounded in real work rather than artificial measures" (Stowell & Tierney, 1995, p. 81). Our students submit multiple, multidimensional indicators for each outcome, thus allowing the assessment of teaching characteristics that are not readily observed with paper and pencil tests, even essay tests. With performance assessment, students must apply and synthesize the principles and concepts they are learning. Important is the rationale statement for each goal in which students must clearly state what evidence is being submitted and why it demonstrates an understanding of the respective outcome. The rationale statements and accompanying evidence indicate understandings and applications that are grounded in the classroom. All of these elements contribute to our belief that portfolios are at least as valid as traditional evaluation procedures.

A Final Thought

When we began using portfolios in our classes, we both had serious concerns about evaluation. We knew it would be time consuming, but we now realize that the time we spend reading and responding is about the same as when we used traditional assessment. We also are relieved to know that we have evaluated hundreds of portfolios without one grade appeal. Based on course evaluations and student conversations, we know our students think portfolios are fair, and perhaps this is the most gratifying aspect of the process.

CHAPTER SEVEN

Quite frankly, at the beginning, I thought portfolios were just another liberal cop-out, but in the end, I kept mine protected as if it were a diary (insecurity, perhaps?).

Ciaran Kelly
This quote by Kelly, a student in the secondary reading methods class and now a teacher in the Czech Republic, is excerpted from his reflections on the portfolio process.

STUDENT ATTITUDES TOWARD THE PORTFOLIO PROCESS

ACENTRAL CONCERN AS we began portfolio assessment was how university students would react to a new approach for evaluating their learning. In general, most have been apprehensive and skeptical. They plead for specific guidelines, such as "How many pages is this supposed to be?" "How many indicators do we need to include?" and "What, *exactly*, do you want?" Student concerns about the portfolio process are certainly legitimate, and no teachers want students to feel insecure or have course evaluations decline because they have failed to adequately allay frustrations. This chapter explores student responses to portfolios, details reactions to personal literacy goals, and offers suggestions concerning the alleviation of student anxieties at the onset of the process.

STUDENT ATTITUDES TOWARD THE PROCESS

By the time they reach teacher training most university students have had considerable experience following detailed course syllabi directions, predicting what professors want, and determining what to do to get a particular grade. The tradition of assigned papers, projects, and exams has long been established, and except for physical education and the arts, criteria for student grades generally have consisted of evaluations that have been other than performance based. Therefore, it is not surprising that preservice teachers are worried about a process that is unfamiliar when they know it will have a direct effect on their grade. In fifth-year credentialing programs, for example, where preservice teachers take most of their methods courses in the semester immediately prior to student teaching, the thought of something so new and different can be very intimidating.

To determine how teacher education students feel about the portfolio process, 64 elementary preservice teachers in a Pennsylvania university and 92 secondary teachers in two California universities were surveyed (Vogt,

McLaughlin, & Ruddell, 1993). All had completed either the elementary or secondary reading methods course in which portfolios were used as the primary means of assessment. Even though the courses differed and some of students were undergraduates (Pennsylvania) and others were postbaccalaureate (California), the portfolio process was consistent in the following ways:

- The assessment was grounded in the respective course's curriculum.

- Students selected their own indicators for each of the learning outcomes.

- Students wrote reflective rationale statements for each outcome and indicator.

- Class and conference times were reserved for peer and student-professor collaboration.

- The professors provided extensive written feedback to each student following both the midterm and final portfolio submission.

During the last regular session for each course, the 156 preservice teachers were asked the following questions:

- How did you feel about portfolio assessment as you began the process?

- How did you feel about portfolio assessment after you received your midterm evaluation?

- How did you feel about portfolio assessment at the end of the semester?

The students' opened-ended responses were coded according to the following categories that emerged from the data: (1) positive comments; (2) negative comments; (3) no opinion; and (4) other. Although the percentage of responses in each category was illuminating (see the table on page 75), the students' written comments were most helpful in understanding their concerns.

BEGINNING OF SEMESTER

At the onset of the process, some of the secondary preservice teachers (19%) expressed positive feelings about the portfolios, such as "I was excited about it"; "It sounded like a good idea"; and "I'm creative so this sounded

Student Attitudes About Portfolios

	Positive	Negative	No Opinion	Other
Question 1: How did you feel about portfolio assessment as you began the process?				
Elementary ($n = 64$)	0%	84%	10%	6%
Secondary ($n = 92$)	19%	70%	6%	5%
Question 2: How did you feel about portfolio assessment after you received your midterm evaluation?				
Elementary	96%	0%	0%	4%
Secondary	89%	3%	0%	8%
Question 3: How did you feel about portfolio assessment at the end of the semester?				
Elementary	98%	0%	0%	2%
Secondary	89%	3%	0%	8%

like fun." In contrast, a majority of both groups (84% elementary; 70% secondary) described negative feelings, using such words as "stressed," "leery," "apprehensive," "confused," "nervous," and "intimidated."

Typical negative comments included the following: "I just couldn't figure out what you wanted"; "I've never done a portfolio and was terrified I'd fail the class"; and "I thought I'd be graded down due to comparison with all the 'artsy' people."

A few students (10% elementary; 6% secondary) stated they had no opinion: "I had never done anything like this before and really didn't know what it was all about. I didn't feel one way or another about it."

MIDTERM

When students had received the first evaluations from their professors, a large majority (96% elementary; 89% secondary) of the preservice teachers expressed positive feelings about the portfolio experience. They indicated they felt "relieved," "encouraged," and "confident." Typical written responses included "I loved it!" "It was lots of work but worth it. Besides, there's no way of cheating"; and "Creativity is not as painful as I thought it would be. I felt confident I could excel even without tests."

Typical negative comments (3% secondary) included "It was very time consuming"; "I wish the portfolios weren't so stressful"; and "It is a lot of pressure. Myself, I'm a test taker."

It is important to remember that students who received the grade equivalent of an *adequate* or below at the midterm were allowed to resubmit revised portfolios.

END OF SEMESTER

By the end of the semester, a majority of the students (98% elementary; 89% secondary) expressed positive feelings about the portfolio process. Typical written comments were as follows: "I feel it is a better way of truly seeing the development of a student throughout a year, rather than just testing"; "It was a great alternative because it really forced me to think about the material and gave me the flexibility to demonstrate my knowledge using my choice of activities"; and "This method of evaluation really required me to evaluate and synthesize the material. In order to demonstrate my understanding, I really had to think, learn, and apply the concepts."

However, not every student enjoyed using portfolios. Although no elementary students expressed negative feelings about the process at the end of the semester, a few (3%) of the secondary students did. They commented, "I would have liked a test"; "I still do not like this at all"; and "I think it encourages procrastination. I also found it annoying that I had to prove my knowledge and come up with a way of proving it."

The students who expressed "other" feelings (2% elementary; 8% secondary) typically stated, "It was a wonderful assessment tool and learning experience, but it was too much in breadth and depth"; or "Portfolio goals were difficult to conceptualize and complete. Yet, completion definitely brought me very positive, even cathartic, insights."

It is interesting to note that no students expressed feelings classified as "no opinion" after they had begun their portfolios. As students began working on them, most appeared to have strong feelings about the portfolio process.

ATTITUDES ABOUT PERSONAL LITERACY GOALS

Our original study, just described, was based on preservice teachers' experiences with course goals related specifically to methods course content. A mini-study was later conducted to determine how students felt about the personal literacy goal and whether it appeared to have value (Vogt, 1994). We wondered if students' feelings and understandings about the portfolio process were enhanced when they set individual literacy goals and submitted relevant evidence for the portfolios. Additionally, we wondered if preservice teachers felt that the literacy goal-setting had implications for their eventual teaching. Typical evidences have included increasing personal or professional reading, regularly reading the newspaper, forming a book discussion group with other teachers in training, and increasing the frequency of written correspondences through letters or e-mail to family and friends.

To determine the value of the personal literacy goal, open-ended questionnaires were given to 74 postbaccalaureate, secondary preservice teachers. Three times during the semester they were asked to describe the literacy goals they had set, the reflecting they had done about the goals, and their overall feelings about creating their own goals. At the end of the semester, they also were asked to describe implications, if any, for their own teaching and to state whether personal goal-setting should be a part of the university portfolio process. All questionnaires were completed anonymously.

BEGINNING OF SEMESTER

During the third week of the semester, students' comments about the amount of time they had reflected on their literacy goals varied. Some expressed they had done a great deal of thinking: "I have done an enormous amount of thinking related to this goal. I first came up with seven areas where I need to improve my literacy! Now, I favor one"; others indicated they had done none: "How much thinking have I done? Zilch!"

Slightly more than half of the students (53%) reported positive feelings about improving their personal literacy, with comments such as, "My initial response was excitement!" "I was happy to have some input as to the requirements for this course"; and "This is the best goal of all!" Others (11%) were mildly interested or apathetic: "My initial reaction was reserved interest"; "I think I am literate enough. After all, I am a graduate student." The rest of the students expressed negative feelings about the goal, stating, "I feel FEAR. I do not want to look within myself and see a problem"; and "My first reaction was something more to do, more work."

MIDTERM

By the eighth week of the course, 64% of the students had clarified their literacy goals and were monitoring their progress. One student explained, "My goal is to increase my personal journal writing to three times per week. I'm marking the days I write on the calendar." Others (36%) expressed that they had clear goals in mind but were not yet collecting evidence to show they were monitoring their progress.

END OF SEMESTER

At the end of the course, students' comments about the personal literacy goal varied. The only common factor (in 33% of the responses) was a concern about the lack of time students felt they had to accomplish their goals: "I like this goal, but wish I had more time to fulfill my true personal literacy goal. I wish the other assigned goals were lessened to enable more time to work on this one."

Twenty-two percent of the responses included comments about the importance of having their eventual students involved in goal-setting. One student wrote, "I think the most important thing I've learned is to help my students set short-term goals which will eventually lead to an ultimate goal."

Seventy-eight percent of the students commented that they had learned things about themselves as a result of setting a personal literacy goal: "I think I've learned that I must develop my own literacy skills and knowledge as well as encouraging my students to do the same. How can I motivate students to read if I'm not doing it myself?"

When asked whether the personal literacy goal should be maintained as a course and portfolio requirement, 94% of the students stated that it should. Two students indicated they thought it should not. One of these students reasoned, "I do not recommend using this goal because it has been a lot of work. It has been good work, but I think it is too much." The other student said, "I don't like the idea of taking responsibility for one's own education."

IMPLICATIONS TO CONSIDER

The personal literacy goal has resulted in some interesting implications to consider:

- Preservice teachers need to be required to think about ways to improve or expand their own literacy.

- Formalizing the goal-setting process appears to be the motivation students need to begin thinking about their own literacy.

- Many students feel great pride in accomplishing basic goals, such as reading the newspaper several times a week.

- The overwhelming majority of students believe that a personal literacy goal is an important course requirement.

- What students learn from the experience of setting and monitoring their own literacy goals extends beyond their teaching to their personal lives.

CHANGES IN STUDENT ATTITUDES

Our research findings and experience have convinced us that portfolio use in elementary and secondary methods courses provides a positive, powerful learning experience for the majority of preservice teachers. We have found few differences in students' responses, regardless of whether they are elementary or secondary, undergraduate or postbaccalaureate. Our findings indicate that most students' feelings about portfolio assessment become more positive as they become engaged in the process. Based on students' written reflections about their experiences, we attribute these changes in attitude to the following:

- Most students experience increased feelings of self-confidence as a result of completing their portfolios.

- Many feel that the extent of the written feedback they receive enables them to see clearly the strengths and weaknesses of the evidence they have submitted.

- Many indicate that collaboration with other students, both in and out of class, enables them to make better choices about what to include for evidence of achieving a goal.

- Many express that they value the opportunity to confer with their professors about their learning.

- Many state they appreciate taking an active role in their own assessment.

- Most indicate they will implement some type of authentic, performance assessment in their own classrooms.

- Nearly all have expressed that the synthesis of their learning is far deeper than that experienced through other kinds of evaluation. Even some students who expressed negative feelings about portfolios also stated their learning was enhanced. One student said in the end-of-semester survey, "I still hate portfolios, but I've never learned so much in a class before."

Our students' attitudes toward portfolios are consistent with other research that has reported preservice teachers' positive responses to the process (McKinney, Perkins, & Jones, 1995; Ohlhausen, 1994). To further build confidence and foster enthusiasm about using portfolios, we have included in our teaching several ways to increase positive feelings.

FOSTERING POSITIVE ATTITUDES

First, as previously described, we provide students with detailed syllabi that clearly describe the course goals, provide possibilities for what evidence to include, establish criteria for evaluation, and explain the grading policy (see Chapter 3 and Appendix B). Also, we bring in journal articles, newspaper clippings, and other evidence of how performance assessment is used in school and university settings in order to place the process within an authentic context.

Second, when we discuss portfolios with our students early in the semester, we talk about possible concerns. These early discussions are dealt with sensitively as we acknowledge student worries and we listen, share, model, and provide class time for discussion. Chapter 3 explained how, during this discussion time, students frequently ask to see portfolio models or samples. We do not show complete portfolios; however, we do show examples of former students' evidence such as a timeline, a piece of poetry, a self-authored book, a cartoon, or ideas from a videotape. These examples appear to motivate and inspire, rather than restrict.

Conference time and availability during office hours are critical for reducing anxiety and frustration. The individual portfolio conferences, described in Chapter 6, also appear to help in clarifying the process.

A FINAL THOUGHT

As portfolio assessment has become widely accepted as a legitimate form of classroom evaluation, students have entered methods classes with more background knowledge of how this type of assessment works. Many are aware of performance assessment because of media reports, personal experiences from substitute teaching, and even from their own children's portfolios. This has tended to decrease anxiety about the process for many students.

However, we believe that a degree of student anxiety about the portfolio process is not only inevitable but important. There appears to be an almost cathartic experience students go through as they determine the appropriate evidence to include in their portfolios. Synthesis of learning is enhanced as they work through the question, "What will best show that I understand and can apply my learning?" One of our students said it best: "It is not enough to read about portfolio assessment, think it is a great, innovative, creative, authentic way to assess students...it needs to be experienced."

CHAPTER EIGHT

As I create, revise, and rewrite my portfolio reflections, I begin to wish that my students were allowed the same opportunity. Not only would I be better able to see them for their gifts and abilities, but they would be able to set goals for themselves and their learning, all necessary elements in becoming successful adults.

Kim Ravese
*This passage by Ravese, a graduate
student in reading education, is excerpted
from her reflections on assessment.*

PORTFOLIOS AT THE GRADUATE LEVEL

WHEN THE PORTFOLIO concept was introduced at the graduate level, students welcomed the opportunity to participate. It offered them greater ownership of their learning and a new role in the student-professor relationship. At the outset, they expressed

- gratitude for acknowledging that after years of study and classroom experience they had more to offer than any examination booklet could show;

- appreciation for the flexibility of the portfolio design because they could set individual timelines to create performances for midterm and final conferences;

- interest in gaining first-hand knowledge of portfolio assessment to facilitate its implementation or further development in their classrooms; and

- excitement and trepidation for the role reflectivity would play in the process.

Student reflections and performances from two courses—"Teaching Reading Through Young Adult Literature" and "Theoretical Models of Reading and Literacy Processes"—illustrate how the dynamic nature of portfolio assessment has stimulated positive change in the graduate reading education program. Prior to the inception of portfolios, these courses were viewed as innovative from curriculum and instruction perspectives and rated very highly by both students and credentialing organizations. Although all courses in the reading program now use portfolio assessment, these courses were selected because they differ greatly. The first course is very practical and uses Kaywell's *Adolescent Literature as a Complement to the Classics* (1993) as its text. The other course is theoretical and uses Ruddell, Ruddell, and Singer's *Theoretical Models and Processes of Reading, 4th edition* (1994). Most students who take these courses are experienced classroom teachers seeking either a master's degree in reading education or reading specialist certification. Student performances from these courses demonstrate the flexible, situated nature of the portfolio process and document changes in the graduate-level teacher education program that have emerged since portfolio implementation.

CHANGES INFLUENCED BY USING PORTFOLIOS AT THE GRADUATE LEVEL

INCREASED STUDENT OWNERSHIP OF COURSE CONTENT

At the start of the theoretical models course, students are often intimidated by the expansive nature of the text. Since the course has become more performance oriented, however, class discussions now abound with references to Ken Goodman, David Pearson, Louise Rosenblatt, Bob Ruddell, and Martha Ruddell as if students were making reference to their favorite authors. As one student noted, "You say that reading our portfolios allows you to walk inside our heads. I understand that concept because we really need to walk inside the heads of the theorists to understand their thoughts. They used to be just names in literacy development. Now, I find myself contemplating their influence when reading professional articles or having theoretical discussions."

PREVALENCE OF TEACHERS AS RESEARCHERS

Since the implementation of portfolio assessment, graduate students are much more likely to perceive themselves as researchers. Documentation of teacher research is common in the portfolios from the young adult literature course because the course is focused on strategies teachers can use to engage their students in literacy. Theoretical models students also report on the implementation of various theoretical frameworks in their teaching. For example, a group of students recently used the Flowers and Hayes (1994) writing model in their classrooms. Before portfolio use, student interaction with course content was viewed more as what would be necessary to know to successfully complete the course.

ATMOSPHERE OF TRUST AND SENSE OF COMMUNITY

One of the most poignant examples of the sense of community that is created among students using portfolios can be seen in the openness students exhibit when sharing their literacy histories. Extremely personal issues such as experiences with insensitive teachers, abusive home situations, homelessness, and life-threatening diseases and their effects on literacy development have been discussed. Each student's views and beliefs are acknowledged and respected.

COOPERATIVE SPIRIT

When students are involved in a challenging process such as developing a portfolio, collaboration can be seen as they negotiate meaning, clarify terminology, and actively contribute to discussions or group projects. It also extends beyond the classroom as graduate students involve fellow teachers and community members in their work.

LINK TO FAMILY LIFE

Students' families make diverse contributions to the portfolio process. When creating their literacy histories and other performances, students often talk with parents, siblings, spouses, and even their own children to gain insights. For example, a graduate student in the theoretical models class investigated the Flowers and Hayes writing model by using writing samples from her daughter's fifth grade portfolio to contrast the model with another view of the writing process. In the young adult literature course, students' family members often engage in discussions about particular young adult titles or participate in dramatized author studies. In the dramatized author studies, graduate students research the life of an author and assume the author's identity to relate his or her life story (McLaughlin, in progress). This offers the students several possibilities for presentation ranging from live performances to videotaped interviews or appearances. Family members often serve as the interviewer or as a character from one of the author's books.

Some unexpected family literacy moments are also shared in students' portfolios. In the evidence that follows, Barbara Seely, a student in the young adult literature course, shares an episode from her family's life that involved one such encounter with young adult literature.

Snowy Night

School had been canceled that day because of the weather. Snow was still falling after supper, and my children were engrossed in their Friday night television routine. Watching them, I remembered a time when evenings like this one were spent with books. There were those early years of reading piles of picture books, followed by the time of easy readers, and finally all of us taking turns with "real" books. At ages 11 and 12, the children had declared independence from family reading, preferring to read alone in their rooms. I missed those times of reading together, and took advantage of a re-run to suggest I read to them instead. After protests that they were not a preschool story hour audience, I did get them settled in for the story. Protests arose over my selection—a chapter from Laura Ingalls Wilder's *The Long Winter*. Resigned to listening to me read something far beneath them, I began.

The chapter was one in which a sudden blizzard surprises the one room schoolhouse on the Dakota prairie. Should the school children and teacher wait out the storm or try to reach home? The school desks might have to be burned for heat—this caught the interest of my listeners. The students and teacher (new to the prairie) start out for town, older students taking charge of younger ones. The description of the cold, snow, and ice particles hooked my listeners. There was some anxiety and nail biting when all sense of direction is lost in the storm, and Cap Garland strikes off on his own path. Relief was on hand, though, when Laura bumps into a building, saving the school from heading out to open prairie, and Cap Garland is found safe in town, having alerted others about the school heading the wrong way.

"Did that really happen?" was the first question. Yes, it did. Other questions followed—about what school was like in the 1880s, about absolute obedience to authority (Laura) or doing what one knows to be right (Cap Garland), and why Mary did not go to school. They found it amazing that provision was not made at that time for a blind child to attend school. They were interested in the many references to Carrie's "peaked" face due to her ill health and wondered what she looked like. My copy of William Anderson's *Laura Ingalls Wilder Country* (Harper, 1990) was on a shelf within reach. We flipped through it, looking at pictures of the Ingalls and the places they lived. Ma, Mary, and Laura looked much the way we thought they would. Carrie, we felt, looked more cranky than peaked, and we found her ill health was probably due to a case of rheumatic fever. Pa, the kids felt, should lose the beard.

And then it was over. We had had a warm time, a return to the past, over all too quickly for me. And for Reed and Holly? A glimpse into the past, both theirs and Laura's, and perhaps, as they watched the storm that night, a time of wondering what would happen if my school were on the prairie and a blizzard came roaring? What would we do? How would it be for us?

Increase in Writing, Discussion, Interaction, and Use of Technology

Portfolios have, without question, increased the amount of thinking, discussion, and writing in our graduate courses. They also have accommodated students' personal strengths by offering multiple ways of to record performances: audiotapes, videotapes, and software complement the written entries.

In the following excerpt from her theoretical models course portfolio, Sheri Lombardi offers an example of how portfolio use has increased discussion among students, as she shares her thoughts concerning a group discussion of literacy histories.

I chose to reflect on our class discussion of literacy histories because I felt I learned a lot about my peers and their views of reading and writing. I also found it enlightening to reflect on my own literacy history because I had never done that before. I realized that my purposes for reading and writing changed as I grew. In addition, I found that there were some teachers and experiences in my life that made a tremendous impression on my literacy development. Understanding the feelings that I had toward reading and writing help me to better relate to the students that I teach today....

Throughout the discussion, I also found that many of my peers held negative or self-conscious feelings toward writing during elementary school because they could not choose their own topics and because it was of such importance to spell all words correctly. This did not help students to become risk-takers.

In addition, I learned that the reading and writing experiences that left the most positive impressions were ones that held strong personal meaning. For example, one classmate recalled a sign she made for her missing cat who later returned. This reinforces the theory that children value reading and writing more when the content presented is somehow linked to their prior knowledge, interests, and feelings.

In conclusion, I found it somewhat ironic that some people who had very positive literacy experiences decided to become teachers because they wanted to share that joy with their own students; others who had very negative experiences also wanted to become teachers because they wanted to share their knowledge and encourage their students to become risk-takers. Although both groups of people had varying literacy histories and chose to become teachers for very different reasons, they now all teach.

Hopefully, their teaching will allow their students to develop positive literacy histories of their own.

INCREASE IN SELF-REFLECTION

Reflections and performances of knowledge and application document each student's learning process. The following poem is a perfect example of this documentation. Dianne Pawlowski had taken the theoretical models course before portfolios were used. She wrote the poem, but there was no assessment format used at the time that would have accommodated her sharing it. She included it later in her "Teaching Reading Through Young Adult Literature" course portfolio as an example of literature response. Taking a suggestion made in her professor's portfolio comments, Dianne sent the poem to *The Reading Teacher*, where it was published. Without portfolios, Dianne's creative, literary response to the reading of Yolen's *Welcome to the Greenhouse* would not have been shared with her professor, peers, or reading educators around the world. The following excerpt and poem is what Dianne submitted as partial fulfillment of a course goal that addresses literacy as an interactive, constructive process.

I guess when I was growing up, I thought reading and writing were as different at science and math. They were usually taught separately. But, in reflecting upon what I've learned in this class, in my other reading classes, and what I've learned through my own teaching experience, I can see that reading and writing cannot exist separately. They both deal with words and meaning. The reader changes the words into meaning and the writer changes meaning into words. In support of this idea, I submit the following piece of writing for you to read: *Greenhouse Revisited*, my own written reaction to reading and other possible writing activities that could be reading-generated.

In my pre-session theoretical models course, Dr. McLaughlin read Jane Yolen's new book, *Welcome to the Greenhouse*. On my way home that evening I started this poem which speaks about how a young school student might feel encountering such a work of literature.

Paradise Found

Our teacher read a book to us
About a far-off land.
She showed us all the pictures, too,
To help us understand.

And as she read the words, her voice
Got loud, then soft and slow.
She made this place sound like a place
Where I would like to go.

My eyes could almost see the green
Of trees that touch the sky.
My ears could almost hear the sharp
And haunting wild ones' cry.

I felt the damp, warm heavy air
That made my breathing slow.
But, it was filled with fragrance, sweet
Of flowers hanging low.

The fruit that grew there tasted great.
Its juice dripped down my chin.
And I was happy walking through
That place that I was in.

When suddenly, I heard my name,
In quite familiar tone.
It made me realize the fact
That I was not alone.

Not only that, but all the trees
Had vanished in thin air.
The sounds and warmth and sweet perfume
Were just no longer there.

My name, again, rang in my ears.
It slapped me in the face.
And there I was, in school again—
Oh, what a dismal place.

But, I'll return to green and wild
To have another look,
As soon as I can borrow it,
And walk into that book.

I certainly wouldn't expect every student to write a poem in response to a story, but a choice of responses would give the students the chance to capitalize on their interests and talents. Some of the choices after reading *Welcome to the Greenhouse* might be to write a story about another habitat, like *Welcome to the Ocean*; a letter to the organization whose address Jane Yolen provides; a letter to Jane Yolen; an interview with one of the animals; a letter to the people who are destroying the rainforest; a research report about one of the rainforest animals.... There are many possibilities in using reading to stimulate writing.

NATURE OF THE STUDENT-PROFESSOR RELATIONSHIP

Since portfolios have been introduced, what used to be professor-student relationships have become student-professor relationships. Graduate students who once were on campus solely for class time, now come early, stay late, and visit campus on days they do not have class to engage in portfolio conversations with professors. These discussions may focus on clarifying some aspect of the portfolio process, exploring the development of a particular evidence, or assuaging portfolio anxieties. Giving this additional time and effort to a course is particularly meaningful for graduate students because many of them juggle family life and full-time teaching positions with their graduate school commitment.

EXTENSION OF PORTFOLIO USE

The high percentage of students in both the theoretical models and the young adult literature courses who have chosen to implement portfolio assessment in their classrooms was unexpected. In support of the Teaching Reading Through Young Adult Literature course goal that addresses instruction across the curriculum, Lisa Balanda, Debbie Wallitsch, Laurie Spalholz, Cheryl Lehman, and Mary Galant chose to work cooperatively to create a thematic unit on individuality. In their rationale statements, the authors reflected on the characteristics of young adults and their roles in society. They noted that individuality had been an important issue in their own adolescence, and they found it to be of equal importance to young adults today. The following excerpt from the evaluation portion of the thematic unit documents the students' thinking about assessment.

A portfolio is a purposeful collection of student work, based on the stated learning goals. The goals are integral to the assessment and evaluation that follow. The student works toward accomplishing these outcomes. It is the teacher's responsibility to match curriculum with assessment. The best method to coordinate this match is through collecting, capturing, and captioning authentic, real-life–like tasks directly from the evidence which indicates a child's growth toward achieving the goals/outcomes.

The purpose of using a student portfolio is one of empowerment. It promotes student self-reflection and self-monitoring as necessary lifelong learning skills. The student is the author of his/her learning, supported by the group which will ultimately benefit from his/her strength. Through portfolio assessment, a student is able to display his/her versatility, refinement, sophistication, growth, and depth of expertise in learning over time. A portfolio contains a variety of performances which teachers and the learner as well as other stakeholders such as parents may use to assess development and to plan experiences which will foster further growth.

Portfolio assessment is student centered, language based, social, and meaningful. The student's knowledge base continually changes and grows and can be accessed for future learning experiences through self-reflection and self-assessment. The development of these life skills fosters the student's self-image as a lifelong strategic learner and as the author of his/her learning progress or journey.

PORTFOLIO ASSESSMENT COMMENTARY

The reaction of the graduate students to the use of performance portfolios has been very positive. Many have chosen to add their reflections to their portfolios. What follows is Chris Berlen's commentary on her portfolio experience in the young adult literature course. She offered her reflection in her portfolio as an evidence for the goal that addresses knowledge and application of instruction, assessment, and evaluation. She was delineating her case for the inclusion of performance portfolios in every classroom.

Reflections of a Portfolio Composer

An interactive process includes the reader, the text, and the context of the reading situation. The reader brings much to the reading task by way of background knowledge and motivation, which greatly influences what is perceived while reading. And so, this invaluable portfolio experience has led me to the realization that not only what my students do is important, but what *I* do is important as well, and can be tapped into when reading to make comprehension clearer or to extend any activity, making all experiences a literacy activity.

Everything I've produced and composed for this YA class has made a lasting impression on me. Each effort from the author presentation to the poetry collection has made me more aware of the value of *doing* in and out of the classroom. It's one thing to have a professor tell you what works in the classroom, and it's another thing to have to actually perform that which is expected of the young adult student.

Each of my performances has had a definite purpose in this course. I know that portfolio assessment works; I know that author presentation works; I know that writing about experience works; I know that reflection and response works; I know that an integrated curriculum works; I know that diversity works; I know that literature-based instruction works; I know that awareness of current developments works; I know that responsibility for composing a portfolio works.

This has been a wonderful course for me, and I'm sure for the rest of the class. In the beginning, it seemed like a lot of work, but now I appreciate the experience I've gained. I feel that I have an awareness of young adult concerns and the confidence with which to welcome them. So many issues, so many questions, so many doubts and problems—so many YA books to read along the way as a guide to sort things out. What a glorious adventure the youth of today have before them. They need not even leave the confines of the classroom or living room. They only need to open the cover of a book.

A FINAL THOUGHT

The graduate portfolio experience has become an ongoing, dynamic conversation that has implications for the university, the home, and the school. In addition to the many benefits the experience has extended to students and professors, it also has led to the continuous improvement of each course and the graduate program as a whole.

PART THREE

PROMISE

Reading to me is like one of those paint machine things at a county fair. You know the one. For 50 cents you put a piece of cardboard into a frame on top of a centrifuge, drop some paint on it, hit the button, and the centrifuge spins the cardboard around until a beautiful, complex pattern, a design is made with the paint. The colors swirl and blend together creating new colors and new patterns.

The reader is the cardboard, that the text, the paint, is dropped upon. The centrifuge, the context, swirls them together until you aren't sure where the paint begins and the cardboard ends. All the swirling is the interaction. Sure, the cardboard is the cardboard and the paint is the paint and the machine is the machine but when and after the interaction takes place, magic happens. That thrill of creation, even momentary, sparks a reaction. That's what reading is to me.

Deborah Costanza
This passage by Costanza, a graduate student in reading education, is excerpted from her reflections on the interactive nature of the reading process.

THE PORTFOLIO EVOLUTION

THIS CHAPTER EXPLORES progressive uses of portfolio assessment from admissions practices to inservice teaching. It begins by describing the use of portfolios for students applying to universities as well as those entering teacher education programs. This is followed by discussion of student teaching and interview portfolios. A collaborative model for inservice teacher portfolio evaluation concludes the chapter. This evolution of portfolio use may be attributed to the fact that in addition to being authentic, multidimensional, reliable, and performance based, this type of assessment is also situated, grounded in the context in which it is being used.

ADMISSION TO UNIVERSITIES

When traditional instruction and assessment were the mainstay of secondary education, the focal points of admission to colleges and universities in the United States were high school transcripts and the results of the Scholastic Assessment Test. These were often complemented by application essays, letters of teacher recommendation, and personal interviews. Now that portfolio assessment is more widely accepted, many institutions of higher education are requiring the submission of portfolios of student work as a component of the admissions process. At some universities, the portfolio supplements the more traditional requirements; at others, portfolios are replacing some of the more traditional measures.

The inclusion of portfolios in admissions practices has been a gradual process that has been met with both positive reviews and realistic concerns. From a positive perspective, portfolios in the admissions process offer more multifaceted and in-depth evidence of students' abilities and accommodate students' learning styles and diverse backgrounds (Vogt, McLaughlin, & Ruddell, 1993). However, there are also valid concerns about issues such as format requirements, the stage in the admissions process when portfolios should be submitted, the training of the admissions personnel, and fairness to applicants who have no prior experience with portfolio assessment.

Although this type of admission requirement allows students to demonstrate their talents in modes other than traditional paper and pencil formats, universities first must face the challenges of implementing portfolio assessment as they try to increase the quality of their admissions processes.

ADMISSION TO TEACHER EDUCATION PROGRAMS

In addition to admittance to a university, students are also concerned with gaining formal admission to a particular undergraduate or graduate program. In using the example of teacher education programs, it is important to note that students often have specific tasks to complete in order to gain admission. For example, many teacher education programs require students to maintain a particular grade point average, successfully complete a personal interview, complete an introductory field experience, write an educational philosophy, pass a mandated basic skills test, demonstrate subject matter competency either through course work or by attaining a predetermined score on a standardized test, pass a speech assessment, submit letters of recommendation, and complete a criminal history check.

In an effort to view the admission requirements in a more innovative and authentic manner, many teacher education programs are now requiring students to submit portfolios to support their candidacy. At some universities the portfolios of student work are being used to replace standardized tests; at others, various criteria for admission to the program are stored within the portfolio as supportive evidence. For example, at the University of California, Santa Cruz, grades and grade point averages are not determined. Instead, written reflections by the student and professors serve as documenting evidence of the student's performance in undergraduate and graduate courses. These reflections could easily be included as portfolio indicators.

Valid use of portfolios as requirements for teacher education programs depends on the evidence students choose to submit and their reflections about it. For instance, a writing sample often is part of standardized measures of competency. It is completed in a specified time period in the context of a test. When using portfolios, however, students are able to submit both formal and informal writing they have created for various courses they have taken. These include works that the students have been able to reflect on and revise.

An additional benefit of using portfolios in the teacher education program admissions process is that students have the opportunity to reflect on their achievements and the reasons they want to become educators. Also, the people reading these portfolios are professors in the teacher education programs who have been involved in the candidacy process. This eliminates concerns about who will review the portfolios and about the need for training and additional funding.

STUDENT TEACHING

Student teaching is what Templin calls "pedagogical schizophrenia" and what Locke labels "pedagogical madness" (in Alvermann, 1981). When students begin student teaching, the transition from the university to the classroom may produce a dissonance that can dilute the influence of university training in as little as two days (Zeichner & Tabachnick, 1981). Many student teachers, struggling just to survive the rigors of daily planning and organizing, also must deal with negative statements from classroom teachers regarding the practicality of university training (Vogt, 1989).

Creating portfolios prior to student teaching that document the learning and application of information acquired during methodology courses may ease the transition from university training to student teaching. The portfolio shows what the student has learned, validates the credibility of the teacher education program, and increases the student teacher's self-confidence.

When students create portfolios during their student teaching assignments, they extend what they have learned in their methods courses to real teaching experiences. As with the methods class portfolio, the student teaching portfolio is goal based. Instructional planning, teaching performance, classroom organization and management, and professional development are often the focus of such goals. Sample evidences include theme and lesson plans, journal entries, feedback from cooperating teachers and supervising professors (such as observational protocols or reflections on discussions), videotaped lessons, a philosophy of classroom organization and management, and summaries of and reflections on professional journal articles and seminars attended. Reflectivity again is a critical factor in the process of developing the portfolio. This further enhances the student's understanding of teaching as a reflective practice and enables the portfolio to evolve over the course of student teaching.

INTERVIEW PORTFOLIOS

The process of hiring new teachers is undergoing change. What used to be accommodated by an application, letters of reference, and an interview has expanded to include evidence of teaching performance. It is not uncommon for school districts to require candidates to submit a portfolio and demonstrate their teaching in either a live performance or on videotape. The interview portfolios include evidence from all phases of the teacher preparation program and may be developed to include artifacts from methods courses and student teaching. Some new teachers may choose to bring an exit portfolio to an interview; this is created during the culminating phase of the program and represents the candidates' best efforts. Goals guiding the interview portfolio development may include demonstration of knowledge of curriculum, teaching performance (subject matter competency and current instructional practices), and classroom organization and management. A philosophy of education often introduces the portfolio.

Unlike portfolios for other educational purposes, the interview portfolio must be succinct. Many administrators have reported that although they value the portfolios, time constraints preclude reviews of lengthy documents. Therefore, the indicators selected to support the goals must be limited. These might include instructional plans; photographs of teaching experiences (such as bulletin boards, classroom design, or interaction with children); brief reflections on current educational practices (for example, early intervention, performance assessment, or cooperative learning); sample curricular designs; a classroom management position statement; and student teaching evaluations. Although a videotape may seem the most appropriate evidence to document teaching performance, many administrators indicate they do not have time to review them. Other districts, however, require live demonstrations of teaching effectiveness. These demonstrations, complemented by the evidence provided in the interview portfolio, add a more realistic and complete view of the candidate's teaching ability.

One unexpected outcome of portfolio use in the hiring process is the number of students who cite their portfolio as a resource in obtaining teaching positions. Administrators have noted that the portfolios serve the dual purpose of documenting the candidate's potential teaching effectiveness and demonstrating his or her knowledge of this innovative assessment practice for use in the elementary or secondary classroom.

INSERVICE TEACHER PORTFOLIOS

Producing positive change in teaching effectiveness is difficult, in part because "teaching is like dry ice at room temperature—it evaporates in front of our eyes and leaves no visible traces" (Shulman in Wolf, Whinery, & Hagerty, 1995, p. 30). Using portfolios provides the opportunity to document teacher performance in diverse ways.

Performance Portfolios for Inservice Teachers: A Collaborative Model (McLaughlin & Vogt, 1995) suggests five categories on which portfolios can be structured: educational philosophy, professional development, curriculum and instruction, student growth, and contributions to school and community. At the onset of the process each teacher develops goals for the five categories that are mutually agreed upon during portfolio conversations held with fellow teachers and administrators. Each teacher also presents a plan for fulfilling the goals. The teacher's plan and his or her progress toward achieving it become the focus of ongoing conversations throughout the portfolio process. Indicators teachers have chosen to support their goals include thematic units demonstrating personal educational beliefs, reflections about seminars and workshops in which they have participated, instructional innovations implemented in the classroom, sample evidences from children's portfolios, and educational programs developed to benefit the community.

Response to the Collaborative Model has been overwhelmingly positive. In fact, it has resulted in the development of a collaborative portfolio model for administrators. Both teachers and administrators agree that portfolio use broadens the evaluation process.

A FINAL THOUGHT

Portfolio assessment for preservice and inservice teachers is being endorsed at state and national levels in the United States. University paradigms are shifting from a teaching to a learning focus (Pennsylvania State System of Higher Education, 1996) and accreditation associations are including portfolios in their call for diverse assessments (Middle States Commission on Higher Education, 1996). Further, in the United States the National Board for Professional Teaching Standards (1989) has begun using portfolios as the assessment model for national certification. The development of portfolios on the teacher education continuum has emerged as a natural process and continues to evolve.

CHAPTER TEN

Could I implement portfolio assessment in the classes I teach without experiencing it for myself? Definitely not. I would not have thoroughly understood the thought processes that a student experiences when creating a portfolio. I would not have realized the importance of designing classroom experiences that allow students to discover what they are learning. I would not have recognized the critical role of reflection in the portfolio process. Finally, without this experience, I would not have internalized my learning, nor felt confident enough to empower my students to take ownership of theirs.

Michele Lloyd
This passage by Lloyd, a graduate student in reading education, is excerpted from her reflections on assessment innovations.

WHERE DO WE GO FROM HERE?

BECAUSE WE BELIEVE authentic, performance-based assessment is an evolving process, we know there are still many questions to be asked and answered about portfolio assessment. We find that each semester we learn something new about this type of assessment, usually as our students create their portfolios. We have become learners with our students as we developed a performance assessment system that works for us.

This chapter presents some of the special insights we have realized as a result of engaging with our students in the portfolio process. We share these thoughts because we believe they are universal benefits to implementing performance assessment in teacher education classes.

INSIGHTS INTO THE PORTFOLIO PROCESS

STUDENT-PROFESSOR RELATIONSHIP

Most of us remember a unique teacher or professor with whom we connected in a special way. Perhaps this feeling was generated because of what we learned in his or her class, because we were challenged and succeeded, and because we had a close relationship with this person. We believe portfolios promote a closer bond between professor and student, perhaps because of their intensely individual and personal nature. Students extend trust more freely during conferences and throughout their portfolio development than they would during assigned projects, lesson plans, or exams. We believe this is primarily because of the goals the students establish and because of the choices of evidence they submit. They are more committed to demonstrate what they know when they have greater ownership of the process.

We also think the deeper level of involvement comes from the nature of the rubric development. Because students are instrumental in determining qualifiers for the rubric designations (such as exceptional or thorough), they want to live up to their own expectations as well as ours.

However, it is the sharing that takes place between student and professor that is the essence of the process. Students offer insights to which we respond.

Our responses promote subsequent dialogue, questioning, and discussion. This give-and-take between professor and student during the portfolio process appears to enrich our relationships with students.

STUDENT RESPONSES TO THE PROCESS

We are encouraged by our students' responses to the portfolio process. While they create portfolios, we have the opportunity to witness the learning process from their perspectives. We see them struggle, hear them voice their pride, and share in how they feel when they talk about what they have learned. The comprehensiveness of the evidence they include demonstrates the synthesis of their learning. Their belief in portfolios and their commitment to using them in their eventual classrooms stimulates our enthusiasm for the process.

This commitment is demonstrated in students' portfolios through assessment plans for their eventual classrooms. For example, in her own porfolio, Mandy Tucker, a secondary art major, included a detailed plan for designing the art class goals, an organizational system for her students' portfolios, and a plan for integrating individual and group reading, writing, and thinking samples. She stated that these "would be intertwined so as to connect the themes and subjects throughout the semester." Her plan indicated not only a commitment to the portfolio process but also the specific ideas about how to implement her own portfolio assessment.

THE DEPTH OF STUDENT LEARNING

While reading their portfolios, we are continually impressed by the depth of our students' understanding. This is obvious in their personal literacy histories, in their individual literacy goals, and in other submissions that support the course content. During the group discussions held after portfolios have been submitted, nearly all students state that they believe they learn more by creating portfolios than they have by taking exams or writing assigned papers. Further, they explain that depth of understanding is necessary because they must apply what they have learned.

CURRICULUM, INSTRUCTION, AND ASSESSMENT ALIGNMENT

Both of us have changed how we plan and deliver instruction since we began using portfolios. Though neither of us favors a traditional lecture model, we have seen our classes develop even more of a student-centered focus as we have released the responsibility for learning to our students. It has been necessary to rethink our curriculum and as a result we are not as concerned about "covering" material as we were previously. Our students are engaged more in exploration and discovery, which has guided our curriculum development. We see alignment among what we teach, how we teach it, and how we evaluate our students' learning and application.

PROFESSIONAL DIALOGUE

One of the most satisfying aspects of the portfolio process has been the ongoing dialogue we have had with colleagues throughout the United States and the world. At the National Reading Conference, the International Reading Association Annual Convention, and the European and World Congress meetings, we have met teachers, administrators, and professors who are involved in designing, implementing, and assessing the effectiveness of portfolios. The thinking of these colleagues has been instrumental in the development of the process we use. Conversations have varied from theoretical issues to management questions to fairness of evaluation procedures. From these dialogues we have learned that our own portfolio process must remain dynamic and responsive to new ideas and models.

A FINAL THOUGHT

As educators, particularly at the university level, we are often in a hurry to determine questions, provide data, make recommendations, and find answers. It is our nature and the result of our training. However, portfolio assessment—from conception to final evaluation—is an intricate and fragile process.

The foundation for this type of assessment has been established at the school, district, state, and national levels. Certainly, we at the university need to be leading the charge, not struggling to catch up. Still, from all that we have learned about the process, we can neither hurry it nor try to formalize it. We believe that the future of this exciting reform effort depends on the teachers of tomorrow who believe in the process, understand its intricacies, implement its elements, and use its results for continuous improvement of the teaching and learning process.

APPENDIX A
ASSESSMENT GLOSSARY

(adapted from McLaughlin, 1995)

This assessment glossary facilitates an understanding of innovative assessment practices. Readers also may wish to use Appendix E and the references at the end of this book as resources for further reading.

Alternative Assessment: Alternative refers to those assessments that differ from the traditional objective response, snapshot type of measures that have characterized the assessment and evaluation of students for many years.

Assessment: Assessment is the gathering and synthesizing of information concerning students' learning (Ferrara & McTighe, 1992).

Authentic Assessment: The authenticity of the assessment rests in its applicability in real life. "The essence of education can be seen in the process of authentic assessment: engaging the students in tasks that are grounded in instruction, that are personally meaningful, that take place in real-life contexts. Logically, authenticity should be the foundation for all classroom assessment systems" (McLaughlin & Kennedy, 1993, p. 7).

Baseline Measures: When students are engaging in performance assessment, they are often working toward specified goals or expectations. Baseline measures are evidences of each goal or expectation that are created when performance assessment is implemented. These measures are evidence of what the students know before instruction begins. The reasoning behind this is that it is necessary to know where each student stands concerning each goal early in the assessment experience so we can measure how each student progresses over time. If we are not aware of what the students know at the outset, we cannot tell how far they have progressed.

Benchmarks: Benchmarks are performance standards against which other performances may be judged (Hart, 1994).

Captions: While some teachers prefer to complete entry slips for performances included in student portfolios, others use captioning. Captioning is the process teachers use to explain why they have selected a particular piece of evidence for inclusion in a student's portfolio. To caption, the teacher writes the purpose of the lesson, the reason(s) for including the work in the portfolio, and which goal the indicator supports. This information is recorded directly on the student's work.

Conferences: Conferences are an invaluable part of the assessment process. In school systems, conferences are often characterized as two-way: occurring between students and teachers; or three way: occurring among students, teachers, and parents. At the university level, conferences usually occur between student and professor or in small groups of students.

Constructivism: In Merseth's 1993 article, Resnick notes that learners construct understandings by building relationships with prior knowledge. Students construct meaning based on these connections when educators focus instruction on broad concepts, encourage student inquiry, value students' perspectives, and assess student learning so that it is contextualized by the teaching (Brooks & Brooks, 1993).

Contextualized or Situated Assessment: Contextualized or situated assessment refers to the gathering of information about students' learning within the learning experience. The term *context* encompasses the purpose of instruction, the mode of instruction, and the setting in which learning takes place (Lipson & Wixson, 1991). Since instruction and assessment are directly linked, this type of assessment reflects the context of the students' learning. Examples of contextualized assessments include attitude/interest inventories, teacher-made tests, projects and text-related activities (Anthony et al., 1991).

Decontextualized or Nonsituated Assessment: Decontextualized or nonsituated assessments are those that do not originate in the learning experience. They are developed outside the context in which they are used. Common examples of decontextualized measures are state assessments (Anthony et al., 1991).

Entry Slips: Entry slips are pieces of paper about the size of a small index card that ask students or teachers to reflect upon the work they wish to include in student portfolios. Students tell which goal their work supports and how it does so. After attaching the entry slip to their work, they set a new personal goal. Teachers tell which goal(s) the performance supports, what the purpose of the lesson was, and what the evidence tells about student progress toward the goal (See Rationale Statements).

Evaluation: Evaluation is making judgments about students' learning. The processes of assessment and evaluation can be viewed as progressive: first, assessment; then, evaluation (Ferrara & McTighe, 1992).

Goals, Expectations, Standards, Outcomes: Goals, expectations, standards, and outcomes are broad statements used to describe what the students will be able to do after learning has taken place. In school systems, there is usually an alignment among course, district, state and national goals, expectations, standards or outcomes. At the university level, there is congruence among course, department, program, and university goals, expectations, standards or outcomes.

Indicators: Indicators are evidence of student performance that support the course or portfolio goals. Student-constructed lesson plans, written essays, observations, interviews, audiotapes, and videotapes are examples of indicators of students' performance.

Observation: Observation plays an important role in performance assessment because it is an ongoing technique that allows the teacher to capture the essence of student performance. Every observation should have a purpose. In the elementary or secondary classroom, the teacher may approach observation by using a clipboard and attaching notes or mailing labels to it. A student's name can be written or printed on the labels with the date and written comments about the purpose of the observation. When the observation is completed, the teacher moves the note or label to a page in the student's portfolio. This facilitates management because as the teacher removes the completed observation forms, it is clear which students still need to be observed. Once the clipboard is empty, the teacher simply refills it. The observations are kept in each student's portfolio in chronological order, offering an ongoing record of student learning.

In the university, professors may choose not to complete systematic observations. However, informal observation of student involvement and participation is often used to enhance later conferences and portfolio evaluation.

Outcomes Assessment: Outcomes-Based Education (OBE) promotes performance assessment that focuses on what the students will be able to do as they exit the school system. These performances are linked specifically to exit outcomes developed by the state or school district (Brandt, 1992).

At the university level, outcomes assessment addresses the congruence between the institution's mission and its performance. The results of the assessment are used to improve teaching and learning (Commission on Higher Education, 1996).

Ownership: Ownership addresses each student's personal involvement with his learning and, in this case, the portfolio process. Each student is encouraged to make the portfolio his own by choosing evidence to include in it, reflecting on how that work supports the assessment goals, and taking responsibility for learning. The students' active role in the assessment process facilitates ownership. Teachers can encourage student ownership of the learning process by involving students in planning, valuing student ideas, and focusing on students' strengths.

Performance Assessment: Practiced in selected educational subjects for many years (such as physical education and the arts), performance assessments now require students to demonstrate what they know in all subject areas. The question is what the students will be able to do at the end of a particular course that will facilitate their achievement of district or university expectations. To document their progress, students engage in performance tasks.

Portfolio Assessment: Portfolio assessment is a type of performance assessment that involves gathering multiple indicators of student progress to support course goals in a dynamic, ongoing process. There are many different types of portfolios. Process portfolios show how the students engage in each stage of an ongoing action. Documentation or descriptive portfolios demonstrate students' progress over time. All of the evidences contained in evaluation portfolios are graded. Showcase portfolios contain examples of what the student deems to be best work. Many educators choose the performance portfolios, which include process, documentation, evaluation, and showcase because they appear to offer the most complete picture of students' learning. These portfolios are purposeful collections of student performance that evince students' efforts, progress, and achievement over time. They are also descriptive and evaluative in nature. They afford us insight into the students' engagement in the learning process and are created through the collaborative efforts of teachers and students. For the purpose of this text, the word *portfolio* refers to the performance portfolio.

In the schools, the contents of the portfolio are usually housed in a pocket folder or an expandable file. In most cases, the portfolios are stored in a plastic crate with hanging files. At the university level, tabbed folders with front pockets or three-ring binders are commonly used.

Portfolio Indexes: This is a list of the portfolio goals or expectations that is placed on the front of each student's portfolio. The goals are stated on the left side of the paper, while the right side is designed with multiple blanks or as a grid. Blanks or boxes in the grid are used to record when a piece of information is placed in the portfolio to support a particular goal. This gives an overview of the portfolio's contents, which also facilitates the conferencing and reporting stages and facilitates portfolio management in the school systems.

Rationale Statements: Rationale statements are explanations university students write for each piece of evidence that is included in a portfolio. They record students' reflections and offer insights to the reader. Students explain clearly what the goal means to them and how the included evidence relates to the particular goal. A rationale statement follows each goal and precedes the indicators of student performance (See **Entry Slips**)

Reporting: News about student performance traditionally has been shared through a written report. With the many innovations in assessment, new thoughts about reporting have also emerged. After implementing performance assessments, many districts redesign their reporting systems to accommodate their assessment goals or expectations. There is currently movement away from traditional letter grades to more detailed descriptors of student performance. This is often manifested in developmental continuums that describe students as "emerging, beginning, developing, or independent." In many districts, these reports complement three-way conferencing.

In higher education, portfolios are usually aligned with the university's grading policies.

Rubrics: Rubrics are descriptions of performance. They are the scoring criteria and generally represent a continuum of performance. Rubrics also facilitate the alignment of portfolios with the reporting process.

Self-Reflection: Self-reflection is a key strategy in assessment and evaluation. It asks students to contemplate what they created, what the experience was like, how they would evaluate their performance, and what new personal goal they could set to perform better in the future.

Syllabus for Teaching Reading in the Elementary School
Dr. Maureen McLaughlin
Pennsylvania State System of Higher Education
East Stroudsburg University

Text: Cooper, J.D. (1993). *Literacy: Helping children construct meaning* (2nd ed.). Boston, MA: Houghton Mifflin.

Course Description: The literacy lesson is the focus of this course. Emphasis is placed on the constructivist nature of literacy, understanding and application of current theory, and the alignment of curriculum, instruction, and assessment. Specific topics addressed include schema theory, inquiry-based learning, authentic literature in the classroom, emergent literacy, strategies and skills, response-centered classrooms, integrated language arts, integrated curriculum, and trends in literacy instruction.

Course Requirements

A. Attendance Policy: Since this course is very hands-on in nature, your attendance and participation are essential. If you are unable to attend a class, please notify me.

B. Readings: Keeping current with assigned readings is integral to successful completion of the course. Such material serves as the basis of discussion as well as informal writings.

C. Assessment and Evaluation Policy: Your performance in this course will be assessed and evaluated through your participation in class and your portfolio. The concepts of portfolio assessment and performance assessment will be discussed in depth at the start of the semester.

Portfolio Submissions

Throughout the semester you will be responsible for creating a performance portfolio. This will serve as the basis for two evaluations: midterm and end of the semester. At midterm, your portfolio will be evaluated on the degree to which you have met the first two goals. Your second portfolio evaluation will occur at the end of the semester. At that time, you will submit materials in the portfolio that demonstrate your knowledge, understanding, and application of the final course goals.

Portfolio Planner

Prior to each submission, you will complete a Portfolio Planner. This will facilitate the organization of your portfolio and will be shared with me two weeks before the portfolio due date. We will conference about your perceptions of each goal and why you have chosen to include particular evidences. I will also offer written feedback at this stage.

Course Goals

The course goals are stated in terms of your performance. By the end of the semester you will be able to demonstrate knowledge and application of

- contemporary theories of literacy instruction;
- authentic literature and its role in the instructional process;
- curriculum, instruction, and assessment; and
- current developments in literacy education.

Performances

For each portfolio evaluation (midterm and end of semester), you will provide performances to demonstrate that you have achieved the course goals. To accomplish this, you will create, collect, organize, and reflect on your evidence for each course goal. Portfolio possibilities may include lesson plans, your literacy history, field experiences, video- or audiotapes, interview data, creative resources (such as an annotated bibliography, poetry anthology, thematic instruction plan, or computer software), a self-authored children's book, or other performances of your choosing.

For example, for the goal addressing current theories of literacy instruction, you might consider the following portfolio possibilities:

- creating your own literacy history, citing the presence or absence of teaching from a particular theoretical perspective and its effects on your literacy development.

- comparing and contrasting the role of constructivism in various models of reading and then planning and teaching a lesson from a particular model's perspective; or

- collaboratively creating a thematic plan from a particular theoretical perspective or redesigning a plan you created earlier to include such a theoretical base.

Please remember that your core evidences should be performances that you have created specifically for this course. If you wish to submit items you have created for other courses or purposes, they are welcome if you can show their relation to a goal, but they will be viewed as supportive evidence.

Rationale Statements

For each goal, a typed rationale statement MUST be included specifying

1. what the goal means to you as a teacher, and
2. how each evidence relates to the goal.

The rationale statement should precede your submission for each goal. It serves as a brief introduction for what you have included. In some cases, depending on the nature of the evidence, the rationale statement may be quite extensive. For other pieces, it may be brief. Keep in mind that the purpose of the rationale statement is to clearly demonstrate your understanding of the particular goal as well as your reasons for including each piece of evidence. The clearer you are in your rationale, the easier it is for the reader to understand your reasoning.

Rubrics

Your portfolio will be evaluated through the use of a rubric based on the following descriptors:

Exceptional
Thorough
Adequate
Inadequate

You and others in the course will have input into the further development of this rubric early in the semester. The final standards will be ones in which we have all had a voice.

In addition, we will occasionally develop rubrics to accommodate specific performances. This not only provides direction to the performance you are creating, but also offers you an opportunity to practice assessment strategies you will use in your classroom.

Further, you will have opportunities to engage in self and peer evaluation. Prior to the submission dates, you will use the rubric we have developed to self-evaluate your portfolio. You will then share your thoughts about that evaluation in our portfolio conversation. You will also be able to engage in peer evaluation prior to each portfolio submission.

Portfolio Conversations

Sharing our thoughts about teaching and learning is integral to the success of our educational experience. Discussion plays an important role both in class and in our portfolio conferences. These conversations have proven invaluable. They afford us opportunities to ask questions, share our thinking, and better understand the learning process. Both individual and small group portfolio conferences will be held during the semester.

Portfolio Construct

From past experience, it appears that the most viable structure for the portfolio is a hardcover, three-ring binder with a front pocket. This accommodates your ability to organize effectively and my need to be able to transport the portfolios to and from the university. Please remember to include your name, section number, phone number, and e-mail address inside the portfolio.

Office Hours: A schedule of my office hours can be found at the start of the syllabus. Please use them to schedule appointments whenever you feel the need. If there is not a mutually convenient time listed, please let me know and we will schedule one. In addition, informal conferences focusing on our assessment plan will be held occasionally during class.

Syllabus for Reading in the Secondary Schools
Dr. MaryEllen Vogt
California State University, Long Beach
Department of Teacher Education

Required Texts:

Ruddell, M.R. (1993). *Teaching content reading and writing*. Boston, MA: Allyn & Bacon.

Vogt, M.E. *Reading in the secondary schools syllabus and handouts*.

Supplemental Text:

Hermann, B.A. (Ed.). (1994). *The Volunteer Tutor's Toolbox*. Newark, DE: International Reading Association.

Course Description: Emphasis on assessment and instruction of individuals and groups in a multicultural setting; textbook selection and evaluation; vocabulary development; comprehension strategies; and the special reading and writing needs of less prepared, of second language, and of accelerated learners. Includes individual instruction of an adolescent and issues of diversity and equity. Traditional grading only.

Course Goals: By the end of the course of study, you will be able to demonstrate knowledge and application of

1. the history of elementary and secondary literacy instruction and the relation between that history and your own literacy development;
2. current theories and principles that support literacy and learning;
3. the interrelation between assessment and instruction in secondary content areas;
4. personal goal-setting for literacy development;
5. assessment and instruction of one or more students who need assistance in any or all of the following areas: reading, writing, study skills, or specific content area learning; and
6. interesting and appealing trade books for middle and secondary school students.

Course Requirements

Attendance and Participation in Class. Regular and prompt attendance at all class sessions is mandatory. Because this is a hands-on class, many instructional strategies will be demonstrated and lecture will be kept to a minimum. Therefore, learning by borrowing someone else's class notes will be nearly impossible. Students will be allowed only one excused absence (giving prior notice to the instructor). Absences thereafter will result in a 10 point reduction in the final grade.

This class requires outside preparation time as well as field work. If you find yourself unable to complete course requirements in a timely manner, refer to the course withdrawal policy and withdrawal dates in the *CSULB Bulletin*. Incomplete grades are infrequently given in this course and are only given for dire emergencies. Becoming "overloaded" does not count as an emergency, so please keep me informed if you are experiencing difficulty in meeting deadlines.

Readings. Assigned readings and Double Entry Journal activities are required each week. Because you will spend a significant amount of time each week in class working from your DEJ journal entries, be sure you have completed them and are prepared to participate in your weekly group.

Portfolio (Goals 1, 2, 3, 4). Throughout the semester, you will be responsible for maintenance of a *course portfolio*. This will be the basis for two evaluations: midterm and end of the semester (see calendar for specific dates). At midterm, your portfolio will be evaluated to determine the degree to which you have met Goals 1 and 2. Your second portfolio evaluation will occur near the end of the semester. At that time you will submit materials that demonstrate your knowledge, understanding, and application of Goals 3 and 4.

The course goals are stated in terms of your performance. For each portfolio evaluation (midterm and end of semester), you are to provide evidence of any type to demonstrate that you have achieved the course goals. To do this, you will gather, collect, organize, and reflect on your evidence for each of the respective goals. Evidence may include extended DEJ entries, lesson plans, information from observations or substituting, audio- or videotapes, interviews, or any combination of these or other materials.

Please remember that your core evidences should be performances that you have created specifically for this course. If you wish to submit items you have created or collected for other courses or purposes, know that they are welcome if you can show their relation to a goal, but they will be viewed as supportive evidence. All written work *must be typed*, except for creative entries (such as posters or collages) and audio- and videotapes.

Organize the material you submit for each goal in the following order:

- *Table of contents.* A list of all the materials included for each of the two submissions. You do not need to include page numbers, just what you are submitting.

- *Tab dividers* separating each goal.

- *Rationale statement.* A typed rationale statement MUST be included, specifying
  a. what the goal means to you as a teacher.
  b. what you have submitted and how the evidence relates to this goal.

This rationale statement should follow the tab divider and precede the materials you have submitted for the goal. In some cases, depending on the nature of the evidence, the rationale statement may be quite extensive. For other pieces, it may be brief. Keep in mind that the purpose of the rationale statement is to explain clearly how each piece of evidence demonstrates your understanding and application of the particular goal. The clearer you are in your rationale, the easier it is for the reader to understand your reasoning. (Note: If you submit materials or notes from other classes or experiences, you need to show how they relate specifically to the content and substance of this course. Do not submit unexplained material.)

From past experience, it appears that the most viable structure for the portfolio is a three-bracket folder with pockets. This accommodates your ability to organize effectively and my need to be able to transport the portfolios to and from the university. Large items (such as posters or artwork that does not fit in the folder) are fine to include separately.

The portfolio evaluation will be determined by how fully and completely you demonstrate knowledge, understanding, and application of the goal. Remember that you (and your students) can best demonstrate competency through multiple indicators, so you may decide to submit more than one piece of evidence of your knowledge, understanding, and application. You are the one to decide what you wish to include and why.

To the extent you are comfortable doing so, I encourage you to use a medium other than expository text for at least one of your portfolio entries (write a poem; create a collage, map, or graphic organizer; design a game, poster, or video). STRETCH! This is an opportunity to let your creative juices flow, but do not worry if you are not a "creative type." The great thing about portfolios is you may do whatever you are most comfortable with and what you feel represents your best effort.

Your portfolio will be evaluated through the use of a rubric with the following descriptors:

Exceptional

Thorough

Adequate

Inadequate

You will have input into the further development of this rubric in the early days of our course. You will all have a voice in the final standards that are established.

The following possibilities may help you in developing your portfolio submissions. Please note that the ideas listed here are simply to stimulate your thinking about the possibilities. You may choose to do any or none of these and you may individually or collaboratively come up with something of your own choosing. Throughout the course, class time will be given to share ideas and discuss possibilities for your portfolios with other class members. You are welcome to work on a goal with a partner or group; simply indicate in your rationale statement the contributions of each group member.

Goal 1: *By the end of the course of study, you will demonstrate knowledge and application of the history of elementary and secondary literacy instruction and the relation between that history and your own literacy development.*

Possibilities: Create a time line or other graphic organizer of historical trends; interview children, parents, grandparents, or former teachers; chronicle your memories about learning to read and write; reflect on your success in subject area classes that required reading and writing in elementary school, middle school, high school, or college; observe current elementary, middle school, and high school subject area teaching, noting in particular the integration of reading and writing activities; extend your DEJs.

To assist you in preparing your literacy history, consider the following (McLaughlin, 1994):

1. What are your earliest recollections of reading and writing?

2. Were you read to as a child? By whom? What do you remember about being read to?

3. Did you have books, newspapers, and magazines in the home? Did you see people using reading and writing for useful purposes?

4. Did you go to the library as a child? If so, what do you remember about going to the library?

5. Can you recall teachers, learning experiences, or educational materials? How did these influence your literacy development?

6. Do you remember reading and writing as pleasurable experiences? If so, in what ways? If not, why not?

7. How did you feel about reading in elementary school? Junior high? High school? Did your reading and writing ability affect your feelings about yourself as a person? If so, how?

8. Are you a reader and writer now? If so, describe yourself as a reader; if not, why do you suppose this is so?

Goal 2: *By the end of the course of study, you will demonstrate knowledge and application of current theories and principles that support literacy and learning.*

Possibilities: Reflect on how you might teach your subject from a constructivist perspective, giving specific ideas for instruction; develop lesson plans that activate and use students' prior knowledge; demonstrate the role of collaboration and social interaction; interview teachers as to their theoretical perspectives; survey current educational software in your subject area to find examples that are theoretically sound; critique and review a lesson you have previously written so that it better reflects constructivist principles; design a poster or cartoon, write poetry; extend your DEJs; observe teachers and determine whether they appear to teach from a particular theoretical perspective—if so, what do you see? If not, what's missing?

Goal 3: *By the end of the course of study, you will demonstrate knowledge and application of the interrelation between assessment and instruction in secondary content areas.*

Possibilities: Determine an assessment plan for your own classroom, including the use of portfolios; interview teachers of your subject area as to how they assess their students; review educational software for your subject area to find examples of how reading and writing are incorporated; plan a management system for your own classroom that is based on cooperative learning groups; describe how you can meet the needs of all students in your classroom, including those acquiring English; have yourself videotaped as you teach your subject to a group of students that includes those acquiring English; determine which reading and writing activities are especially appropriate for your subject area; include your lesson plan from this class with reflections as to what worked, what did not, and why; observe teachers in your subject and reflect on their integration of reading and writing activities; attend a conference or workshop session dealing with reading and writing integration; read, summarize, and reflect on a literacy or sheltered English article in a professional journal; observe and reflect on a bilingual or sheltered English lesson; extend DEJs.

Goal 4: *During the course of study, you will demonstrate knowledge and application of personal goal-setting for literacy development.*

Possibilities: Develop a system for organizing articles from a professional journal in your subject area; schedule a regular time for newspaper reading each day; learn to access and use resources on the Internet; learn to send and receive e-mail; build time into your schedule for pleasure reading; improve your vocabulary; write letters to friends and family; organize a reading discussion group for teachers; set up a schedule for reading aloud to your own or neighborhood children; or record your progress in keeping a daily journal.

Goals 5 and 6 relate to the required field experience and to young adult literature. A description of these goals follows:

Goal 5: *By the end of the course of study, you will be able to demonstrate knowledge and application of assessment and instruction of one or more students who need assistance in any or all of the following areas: reading, writing, study skills, or specific content area learning.*

The purpose of the field work is to provide you with experience in applying the assessment and instructional strategies learned in this course, to assist you in becoming a reflective teacher, and to provide tutorial assistance for an adolescent (or group of two to four adolescents) in a middle or secondary school. You will meet with your student(s) for 12 hours during which you will informally assess reading, writing, and study skills, and assist your student in becoming a more strategic learner in content classes. You may use a variety of materials, including ideas from the text and handout packet, as well as your own ideas gleaned from the assessment of your student's interests and abilities.

At the conclusion of your tutoring, you will submit the following:

- A description of the tutee(s), including first name, age, grade level, and school;

- A summary of assessment findings, including interests, estimated reading levels, writing abilities and needs, and strategy use;

- A summary of instruction, including specific strategies and activities you taught;

- A written reflection on the tutoring experience, including what you learned about your tutee(s) as well as what you learned about teaching and learning;

- Your recommendations for your tutee(s) regarding future instructional needs; and

- Copies of Reflection Logs, assessment papers ("protocols"), and all student work.

Goal 6: *By the end of the course of study, you will be able to demonstrate knowledge and application of interesting and appealing trade books for middle and secondary school students.*

The purpose of this requirement is to familiarize you with current adolescent and young adult literature and to enable the class to create an annotated bibliography of books appropriate for teenage readers. Read and annotate one current (written within the last 10 years) piece of fiction or nonfiction especially created for young adults. Models for the annotation can be found in the handout packet. For the last class session (during finals week), you will bring copies of your annotation for each class member and read a selected passage (150–200 words) to a group of fellow students. Either copy the selection you will read aloud or save the book to read from.

Evaluation

On the basis of the portfolio evidence you submit, your tutoring reflections, the annotation, and your participation in class, you will earn points for demonstrating your understanding and application, that when totaled, will be used to compute your final grade for the course. Points for each goal are as follows:

Goal 1: 20 History and trends of literacy instruction

2: 15 Theories of literacy instruction

3: 30 Assessment and instruction

4: 10   Personal literacy goal

5: 20   Tutorial fieldwork

6: 5   Book annotation

The final grading scale is:

A = 92–100
B = 83– 91
C = 75– 82
D = 64– 74
F = 0– 63

Please note: If your portfolio is submitted past the due date, you will be docked five (5) points for each late submission. Absences will be recorded, and if there is more than one absence, 10 points will be deducted from the final grade. It is expected that all students will participate in DEJ and whole class discussions.

APPENDIX C
EXAMPLES OF EVALUATION SHEETS

The following are representative evaluation sheets we have returned to students after reading their portfolio submissions. Because each student's work is individualistic, so too is each evaluation sheet. To illustrate the diversity of student performances, examples of differing levels of student achievement are included for each course.

Teaching Reading in the Elementary School

Portfolio Submission 1   **Spring**
Name: XXXXXXX

Goal 1: Knowledge and application of contemporary theories of literacy instruction.

	Exceptional	Thorough	Adequate	Inadequate
Indicator 1	X			
Indicator 2	X			
Indicator 3	X			
Overall submission	X			

When reading your portfolio, the words "insightful" and "creative" kept coming to mind. You seem to have a keen understanding of the literacy theories we've studied. The lesson plans you created based on *The Three Little Pigs* theme thoroughly illustrated the constructivist influence you were hoping to achieve. Your students will appreciate the concern for their ideas that you've demonstrated throughout the activities. Creating a video that analyzed your literacy history from the theoretical perspectives of three of your former teachers was absolutely fascinating. I agree that many educators fail to realize the profound influence of their teaching. Please see my additional comments in your portfolio.

The performances and reflections you've included clearly demonstrate that you have attained this goal. What a fabulous beginning!

Goal 2: Knowledge and application of authentic literature and its role in the instructional process.

	Exceptional	Thorough	Adequate	Inadequate
Indicator 1	X			
Indicator 2	X			
Indicator 3	X			
Indicator 4	X			
Overall submission	X			

You will notice that I have made extensive comments in your portfolio concerning your indicators for this goal. Each evidence is simply phenomenal! Your students will be so fortunate to have you as a teacher. The depth of your rationale statements and the quality of each performance, especially the book of poetry that you created, were, as the chart says, exceptional.

Teaching Reading in the Elementary School

Portfolio Submission 1   **Spring**

Name: XXXXXXX

Goal 1: Knowledge and application of contemporary theories of literacy instruction.

	Exceptional	Thorough	Adequate	Inadequate
Indicator 1			X	
Indicator 2			X	
Indicator 3				X
Overall submission			X	

As we discussed in our conference, your performances have potential, but this is not evidenced by the quality that appears in your portfolio. This work is adequate at best. As I indicated in our conference, I will be happy to re-evaluate, if you choose to resubmit these goals. However, as things stand now, I can only tell you that what you've submitted does not do justice to the ability you have shown in class throughout the first eight weeks. Please see specific comments throughout each evidence.

Goal 2: Knowledge and application of authentic literature and its role in the instructional process.

	Exceptional	Thorough	Adequate	Inadequate
Indicator 1			X	
Indicator 2		X		
Indicator 3			X	
Overall submission			X	

The annotated resources that you created for use in the third grade classroom are very well developed. This evidence is much more compatible with what I had expected from your portfolio planner. Concerning your other submissions, please see the detailed comments included in your portfolio.

Reading in the Secondary Schools

Portfolio Submission 2   **Spring**

Name: XXXXXXX

Goal 3: Knowledge and application of assessment and instruction.

	Exceptional	Thorough	Adequate	Inadequate
Authentic assessment	X			
Reading and writing	X			
Cooperative learning	X			
Sheltered English	X			
Overall submission	X			

Points: 30/30

You are such a joy to have as a student! You make me feel so good! This is a wonderful submission! Your assessment overview is right on target—and authentic assessment, as you said, is a natural arena for home economics. All of you "hands-on" teachers have been doing this for years! The lesson you designed is close to perfect—it has all the elements for successful experience for kids—those for whom learning is easy and those who struggle. The sheltered English techniques which are built into the lesson are right on target. The nutrition unit is spectacular—I certainly hope you were able to get credit for this in another class and didn't do *all* this for 457! Last, I love the use of the children's literature—what integration! In all, it's great!

Goal 4: Knowledge and application of setting a personal goal.

	Exceptional	Thorough	Adequate	Inadequate
Goal, Plan, & Progress	X			
Reflections	X			

Points: 10/10

Again, what you have submitted certainly goes "above and beyond." Just deciding to read a weekly journal article (and you've chosen some fine scholarly journals) is an ambitious goal, especially with your other coursework and family responsibilities. But, you certainly reached your original goal and then some. I'm delighted to see you determined to integrate reading, writing, listening, and speaking into home economics teaching and the ideas you've suggested in your reflective summaries are great. Perhaps you'll eventually be unable to keep up this pace with your journal reading...but it does appear a life long habit has been begun.

I have really enjoyed having you in class this semester. If I ever came into class a bit frazzled (more often than I'd like some days!!), you always buoyed me up. You have such a bright future in teaching. Best wishes and please keep in touch!

Goal 5: Knowledge and application of assessing and teaching an individual or small group.

	Exceptional	Thorough	Adequate	Inadequate
Assessment	X			
Instruction	X			
Summary	X			
Reflections and recommendations	X			
Overall submission	X			

Points: 20/20

On your interest inventory, you said you like to do well in your classes—no kidding! This is another beautiful submission. Vu was so lucky to have you as her teacher —as will be all your future students. Your work with her appears so appropriate and sensitive to what she needs. The lessons you included as well as all the supplementary materials you created for her are indeed impressive. Wow, what a submission!

Portfolio Submission 2 **Spring**

Name: XXXXXXX

Goal 3: Knowledge and application of assessment and instruction.

	Exceptional	Thorough	Adequate	Inadequate
Authentic assessment		X		
Reading and writing			X	
Cooperative learning				X
SDAIE				X
Overall submission			X	

Points: 25/30

First off, your overview of standardized testing is very complete—I'm not clear as to your feelings (or knowledge) about more authentic types of assessment, e.g., portfolios, since you didn't really discuss them. The lesson plan, while fine for good readers and fluent English speakers, will be very difficult for students who struggle to learn as I don't see any provisions for adapting the text—you're just expecting them to "read" it—and many will be unable to do so. I'm curious as to why you didn't incorporate any reading strategies from class—especially for the reading phase. This lesson needs more thought if kids are to be successful with it. Whereas you mention SDAIE, from what you've presented, I'm not convinced you understand the concepts or specific strategies to use for LEP kids. You may wish to brush up on all this prior to student teaching.

Goal 4: Knowledge and application of setting a personal goal.

	Exceptional	Thorough	Adequate	Inadequate
Goal, Plan, & Progress		X		
Reflections	X			

Points: 10/10

I'm glad this was a personally fulfilling goal for you and that you accomplished what you set out to do. The courts are lucky to have someone as caring as you to work with troubled teens!

Goal 5: Knowledge and application of assessing and teaching an individual or small group.

	Exceptional	Thorough	Adequate	Inadequate
Assessment	X			
Instruction		X		
Summary/Reflections			X	
Overall submission		X		

Points: 17/20

It's clear you understand the nature and purposes for tutorial work. However, I'm left wondering exactly what you did each time you were with the boys. I don't know what you mean by "interview" and I'm not clear how you can do that for two full periods, so I'm feeling a little frustrated! Also, you haven't included here what YOU learned from all this—the "philosophy" gives a global look but not a personal reflection. What did you gain from this tutoring experience? What did you learn about yourself as a teacher? Please remember to turn in your tutoring verification form.

APPENDIX D
ADDITIONAL STUDENT
PERFORMANCES

Mary Ann Ley, a student in the secondary reading methods course, submitted "Walk Through Memory Lane" as evidence of her understanding and application of the history of literacy education in the United States. Along with the poem and description of the various time periods, she also used a CD ROM to access additional information and pictures, which she converted to hard copy. The pictures included a *Horn Book*, the *New England Primer*, and several photographs of classrooms throughout the last two centuries. Her use of Dick and Jane as central characters, beginning with Mr. Jones and Mistress Smith and ending with Ricardo and Janelle, is especially creative.

Rationale Statement

Books are some of my best friends. They have inspired, informed, and entertained me. Some of them make me laugh, some of them make me cry, and some of them take me on adventures that are exciting and magical. As a teacher, I would wish this friendship for all my students.

Understanding the educational and literary environment that helped shape my families' literacy is explored in See Dick and Jane Walk Down Literacy Lane. Understanding how I developed this passion for books is explored in My Personal Walk Down Literacy Lane.

Walking down these two "lanes" has helped increase my awareness of the importance of an environment that plants literacy seeds. As an art educator, I hope to create art classrooms that motivate and inspire personal literacy related to art production, criticism, aesthetics, and history.

nce upon a time, two children, named Dick and Jane,
Wanted to walk down Literacy Lane,
And learn how to read, more than just their names,

But a teacher told them they had to read—see, walk, and run,
Before they could have any real reading fun.

So they saw Dick walk and they ran with Jane,
And read a story about Tip, that was very plain.

They tried phonics and sight words and Basals galore,
And found it all—an incredible chore!

Why learn how to read such mundane stuff?
Stories about Spot were primarily fluff!

So they closed their books and said they wouldn't read,
When a teacher said, "Wait, I've got just what you need."

"Away Primers, McGuffeys, Hornbooks, and Slates,
I've got exciting stories that are really quite great!"

Dick and Jane were not too sure that they wanted the book,
But they began to read literature and were suddenly hooked.

They read and they read on into the night,
And finished the book upon the dawn's early light.

After that book, Dick and Jane learned how to read and write,
And because they are literate, their future is bright.

The moral of the story when learning to read,
Find a good book to plant the literacy seed.

–Mary Ann Ley

Mr. Jones and Mistress Smith from 1600-1840 went to Dame Schools. They were taught reading, writing, arithmetic, and religion. Most learning was memorization, which was stimulated by whipping. Mr. Jones and Mistress Smith though barely seven were viewed as mini-adults. They read the scriptures and the Lord's Prayer out of the Horn's Bible. They learned their alphabet from the New England Primer, the first basic textbook. The main influence on education was the church.

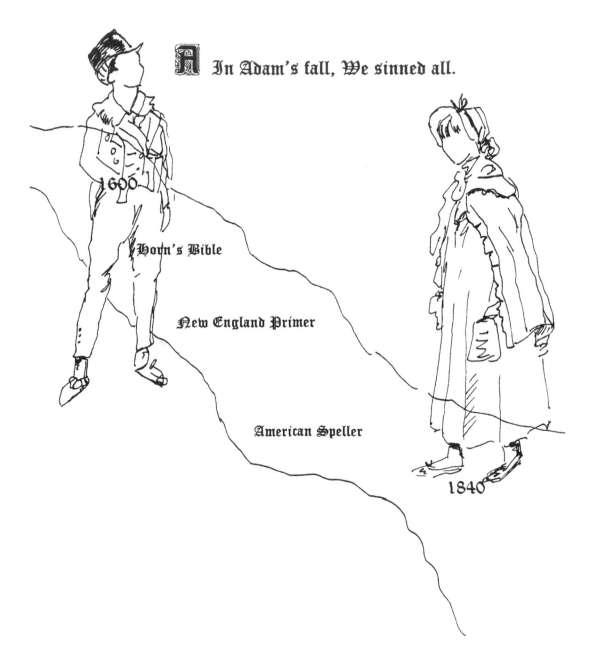

In Adam's fall, We sinned all.

1600

Horn's Bible

New England Primer

American Speller

1840

Master Richard and Miss Martha Jane from 1840-1910 went to the common school which began in the 1820's. Horace Mann was the secretary to the Massachusetts state board of education and promoted educational reform. The rise of industrialism and capitalism with many new inventions demanded new kinds of knowledge. Scientific instruction became more important than the classics. Master Richard and Miss Martha Jane used slates and the McGuffey Readers which appeared in 1836. Webster's American Spelling Book promoted the spelling bee competitions and the ever popular New England Primer still instructed readers in moral virtues. Master Richard and Miss Martha Jane had to memorize many sayings like this:

Work while you work, play while you play.
One thing each time, that is the way.

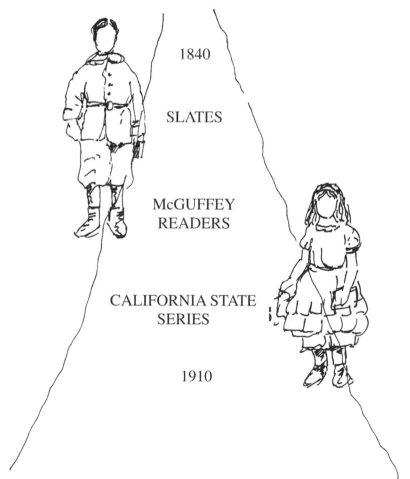

1840

SLATES

McGUFFEY
READERS

CALIFORNIA STATE
SERIES

1910

Richard and Mary Jane from 1910–1950 went to schools influenced by immigration and World War II. John Dewey's influence in the 1920's and 1930's instigated a collision of new and old ideas in the classroom. Dewey maintained that the mind and its thinking processes are developmental and that the stages of growth and knowledge vary from stage to stage. At the same time the "testing" movement was gaining momentum. During the 1920's, IQ and achievement tests were first given on a wide scale. Basically, there were the "progressive" Dewey educators trying to maximize a child's ability to think while the conservatives or essentialists wished to focus on tests of memory. Richard and Mary Jane learned phonics, sight words, and were the products of tracking.

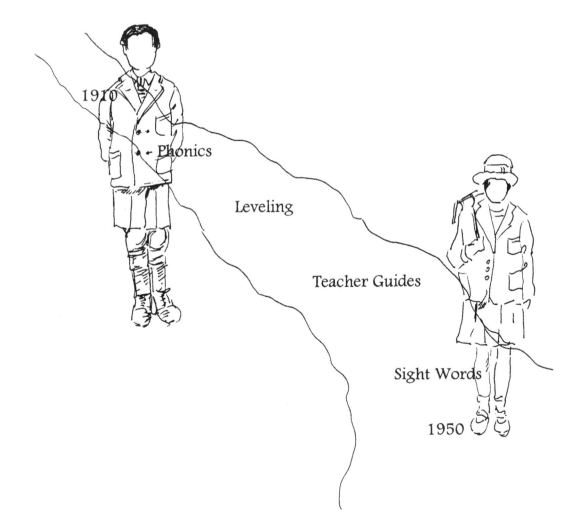

Dick and Jane attended public schools from 1950-1985. The sending of the first space satellite, Sputnik in 1957 by the Russians, launched the American public educational system into an orbit of its own. Conservatives alleged that the cream puff pedagogy of 40's had led to the decline of traditional curriculum in school programs. There was an insistence on performance and excellence that increased academic pressure and renewed interest in testing and national assessments. Dick and Jane read from their Basal Readers and lead a rather conservative and structured homogenous life. "New math" and "new science" became synonymous with the emphasis on cognitive performance and curriculum reform. Technological revolutions, separation of Church from state, Civil Rights and busing influenced the atmosphere of the schools, but the method of instruction was still predominantly teaching by telling, rather than by doing. Dick and Jane read:

```
See.  Dick.  See Dick.  Run.  See Dick run.
See.  Jane.  See Jane.  Run.  See Jane run.
See.  Dick and Jane.  See Dick and Jane.
See Dick and Jane run.
```

Basal Readers   Magazines &   Film
              Tapes   Strips

Ricardo and Janelle started school in 1986 and attend a multi-cultural, bi-lingual school that promotes inclusion or equal opportunity for all children. Downsizing, redefinition of the family, influx of immigrants, and telecommunications are some of the influences that are shaping their education. Cooperative learning has minimized the competitive thrust while portfolio and authentic based assessment are their guides into the new century. The curriculum is student centered and integrates reading, writing, listening, and speaking to promote critical thinking and problem solving. Ricardo and Janelle no longer learn to read by rote, phonics, or sight words. Teachers use a balanced literature approach that combines phonics, semantics or meaning, and syntactic or structure to cue assimilation and accommodation. Ricardo and Janelle experience the joys of reading real literature or "realia."

I do so like
green eggs and ham!
Thank you!
Thank you,
Sam-I-am!
        -Dr. Seuss, *Green Eggs and Ham*

Literacy Lane

R e a d i n g   F u n

F o r

E v e r y o n e

The following example shows a detailed rationale statement. Karen Lund, a student in the "Teaching Reading Through Young Adult Literature" course, included this information to introduce the performances she created to support her understanding and application of current developments in literacy instruction. Indicators to support this goal included a dramatized author study, an annotated bibliography of contemporary young adult novels, a thematic instructional plan about Japan created with a group of her peers, lesson plans focusing on poetry for young adults, and reactions to articles from professional publications.

Rationale Statement

I feel that much of what I've learned in this course applies to this goal. I will explain my reasoning by reflecting on selected evidences I developed throughout the course.

Creating the author study compelled me to think of the importance of using books which really engage the students and keep their interest. The author study did not just help me to learn about the author's life, but her style and purpose. This made me realize that if everyone really thought about what makes a real book real, they would be using authentic literature and designing activities like the author study that promote students' thinking.

By reading articles like "The Birth of Holden Caulfield" and "Huck Finn Reconsidered", I could see the problems some people may have had with using certain titles in their schools, but frankly, with everything children are experiencing outside the classroom these days, I can't figure out why Huck Finn, Holden Caulfield, and other characters upset people so much. We don't have a banned book list at our school, and I hope we never do. It was a surprise for me to read articles in which people get so enraged about these, in my opinion, harmless books. If we use this type of book and discuss it, we are teaching our young adults to think. Holden's story is one of a young man entering adulthood. He isn't on a smooth road, but our students aren't going to flunk out of school, curse, and run away just because they read a novel.

The young adult annotated bibliographies that we chose to create have become hot reading in our teacher's room. I have gotten some wonderful ideas for books to use from this and without the benefit of seeing what others created, I would only have known about my five books. This is a current topic because if we are going to include literature across the curriculum, then we need to know what is out there.

The thematic unit is current, not because it is a new instructional technique, but because we refined it to make it more effective for our contexts. The strategies I learned in this course will really expand what I have done in the past with thematic plans. Also, by creating the themes cooperatively we learned how easy or difficult it can be to work with different people. We ask our students, "Why aren't you finished?" Well, sometimes we need to work with people to remember how hard it can be to get a group moving in the same direction.

Poetry is hot. Every workshop flyer that winds up in my mail box is about poetry. What is important to this goal is that the way we plan the poetry lessons with motivational and extending activities will encourage the students to stay involved and stay excited about this genre. Like the example you read in class, students' feelings for poetry can depend on how we, as teachers, present it.

The instructional techniques may not sound new, but they are. For example, in our work with *To Kill a Mockingbird*, there were many choices we could integrate in our teaching: the diverse types of reading, the use of literature logs, group discussions asking for students to document their thinking, using video tapes to compare (as the article "From Page To Screen" pointed out) what happens to the book when it becomes a movie, and newspaper articles to bring a current perspective to a topic. In addition, the use of a classic core novel in conjunction with contemporary young adult titles exposes students to multiple perspectives that are thematically linked.

Teachers of young adults should let the students think, let them explain what they feel, understand, and don't understand. As noted in the article, "Introducing Teens to the Pleasure of Reading," young adults need a sense of ownership to really become engaged and love what they are reading. This article also promoted a community of readers, challenging students to generate their own insights and make personal connections.

Current developments can't ignore the type of material out there for our young adults. "Today's YA Writers: Pulling No Punches" made it very clear that the literature available to me as a young adult is very different from what is available now. My mother may not have wanted me to read books about gays, teens having babies, or drug use when I was a kid, but I did anyway. Podl's article said so few teens read for pleasure that it is almost an oxymoronic phrase to them. It's clear that young adults don't want to read about people who look and act like their parents- they want the emotionally powerful books that YA literature offers now. This diversity of young adult literature may just get our teens "reading for pleasure."

In this personal history, Joanne Deardorff recounts her literacy experiences. Deardorff, a student in the "Teaching Reading Through Young Adult Literature" course, details her literacy as it emerges from the role of student to the role of teacher. This was submitted as one of the evidences to support her understanding and application of historical perspectives of literacy.

I Remember...
A Literacy History

I remember receiving "Golden Books" as presents and having my dad write my name in them in his "drafting style" printing.

I remember being read to and always thinking it was not enough.

I remember sitting on my dad's lap on Sundays as he read the comics to me.

I remember winning my first prize at the York Fair for a "first grade" picture of my family in which I drew everyone with very long legs and short bodies.

I remember writing exercises involving large lined yellow paper, a thick pencil, and low grades.

I remember a feeling of pride when I was allowed to bring my "Dick, Jane, and Sally" readers home, so I could read to my dad and having to repeat each page to him on which I made a mistake.

I remember wanting to read ahead and being aware that Mrs. Shoemaker, who had said "no," would know.

I remember the fun I felt as I bought new books and could write my name and the date inside them.

I remember reading collections of poems and enjoying their rhythm and cadence.

I remember reading in a reading circle during lunch/recess and being told I read too dramatically, yet knowing that was what my dad wanted to hear.

I remember reading collections of fairy tales and being able to visualize the stories.

I remember trips to the York City Library to choose as many books as I could and being fascinated by the water fountain and pool in its lobby.

I remember reading music for piano lessons on a piano bought from an "old maid" school teacher who lived in West York.

I remember sanding, staining, and using my wood burning set to complete a "plywood" cover, which my dad had cut, for my *Great Expectations* notebook.

I remember lying on the sofa on Saturday mornings and reading *Lassie Come Home*, *Rin Tin Tin*, and *Black Beauty*, yet knowing fully that my mother expected me to run the sweeper, dust the furniture, and do the dishes.

I remember writing in a diary, wanting my handwriting and my spelling to be perfect.

I remember not wanting to read Nancy Drew or the Hardy Boys because they were mysteries.

I remember reading all I could find for a Daughters of the American Revolution essay contest and feeling so good about all I knew.

I remember finding time before school during my senior year to use a reading machine to increase my reading speed and comprehension.

I remember feeling out of place as I read my third place Daughters of the American Revolution essay which was filled with facts.

I remember hiding *Lady Chatterley's Lover* as I read and not talking to anyone about the whirling feelings I was experiencing as I visualized their passion.

I remember writing Haiku with my twelfth grade student teaching class and feeling totally engrossed in my writing.

I remember my students' progress during my "book of the month" club readings as they groaned in September.

I remember writing poetry during my "duty" period of in-school suspension and knowing that the time was flying right along for me, but not for the other students.

I remember for many years only reading the material I was teaching.

I remember my students asking in December when we would be going to the library for the next "book of the month."

I remember reading Dr. Seuss's *Hand, Hand, Finger, Thumb* so often to my younger daughters that I had memorized it.

I remember the overwhelming feeling I had as I read The Awakening for the first time.

I remember being concerned that I would not be able to keep up with the reading for graduate school, when I first saw the syllabus for a critical interpretation class.

I remember the thrill and frustration I felt as I read the table of contents for Norton's *Anthology of Literature by Woman Writers*.

I remember coming to the realization when I started my thesis on Edith Wharton that I had a slow, deliberate method of taking notes.

I remember writing my own folk tale hero adventure about a "princess" of the Delaware Water Gap and being told to drop out the two things that I thought had to be in my story.

I remember the anger I felt as I read *Beyond Power* by Marilyn French and *Backlash* by Susan Faludi.

I remember the satisfaction I felt as I received a Geraldine R. Dodge Foundation Summer Opportunity Award for a proposal to read literature by writers of diverse backgrounds.

I remember the feeling of calm and satisfaction I experience every time I walk into a bookstore, even if I am only browsing.

I remember many students asking the same question each year— "Why must we read?"—and hoping that reading will become a source of adventure and intrigue for them as it is for me.

APPENDIX E
SUGGESTED READINGS

In addition to the references listed at the end of this text, we have found the following resources valuable to our understanding of innovative assessment practices:

Alexander, F. (1993). National standards: A new conventional wisdom. *Educational Leadership, 50*(5), 9–10.

Anderson, J., DuMez, J., Hunter, A., McLaughlin, M., Peter, M.G., & Vogt, M.E. (in press). *Professional portfolios for teachers.* Norwood, MA: Christopher-Gordon.

Au, K., Sheu, J., Kawakami, A., & Herman, P. (1990). Assessment and accountability in a whole literacy curriculum. *The Reading Teacher, 43*, 574–578.

Belanoff, P., & Dickson, M. (1991). *Portfolios: Process and product.* Portsmouth, NH: Heinemann.

Calfee, R.C., & Perfumo, P. (1993). Student portfolios: Opportunities for a revolution in assessment. *The Elementary School Journal, 90*, 337–349.

Camp, R. (1990). Thinking together about portfolios. *The Quarterly of the National Writing Project and the Center for the Study of Writing, 12*(2), 8–14, 27. Berkeley, CA: University of California.

Costa, A.L. (1989). Reassessing assessment. *Educational Leadership, 46*(7), 2.

Feuer, M., & Fulton, K. (1992). The many faces of performance assessment. *Phi Delta Kappan, 74*(6), 478.

Graves, D., & Sunstein, B. (1992). *Portfolio portraits.* Portsmouth, NH: Heinemann.

Harp, B. (1991). *Assessment and evaluation in whole language programs.* Norwood, MA: Christopher-Gordon.

Herman, J., Aschbacher, P., & Winters, L. (1992). *A practical guide to alternative assessment.* Alexandria, VA: Association for Supervision and Curriculum Development.

Herman, J., & Winters, L. (1994). Portfolio research: A slim collection. *Educational Leadership, 52*(5), 48–55.

Meyer, C. (1992). What's the difference between authentic and performance assessment? *Educational Leadership, 49*(8), 39–40.

Murphy, S., & Smith, M. (1990). Talking about portfolios. *The Quarterly of the National Writing Project and the Center for the Study of Writing, 12*(2), 4–7, 24–27. Berkeley, CA: University of California.

O'Neil, J. (1992). Putting performance assessment to the test. *Educational Leadership, 49*(8), 8–13.

O'Neil, J. (1993). Can national standards make a difference? *Educational Leadership, 50*(5), 4–8.

Paulson, F., Paulson, P., & Meyer, C. (1991). What makes a portfolio a portfolio? *Educational Leadership, 48*(5), 60–63.

Shepard, L. (1989). Why we need better assessments. *Educational Leadership, 46*(7), 4–9.

Simmons, J. (1990). Portfolios in large-scale assessment. *Language Arts, 67*(3), 262–268.

Sizer, T., & Rogers, B. (1993). Designing standards: Achieving the delicate balance. *Educational Leadership, 50*(8), 24–26.

Stiggins, R. (1991). Assessment literacy. *Phi Delta Kappan, 72*(7), 534–539.

Valencia, S. (1990). Alternative assessment: Separating the wheat from the chaff. *The Reading Teacher, 44*, 60–61.

Alvermann, D.E. (1981). The possible values of dissonance in student teaching experiences. *Journal of Teacher Education, 32*(3), 24–25.

Anderson, R. (1995). *Encouraging all voices to be heard: Constructing collaborative student teacher portfolios.* Paper presented at the 45th Annual Meeting of the National Reading Conference, New Orleans, LA.

Anderson, R.C. (1994). Role of the reader's schema in comprehension, learning and memory. In R.B. Ruddell, M.R. Ruddell, H. Singer (Eds.), *Theoretical models and processes of reading* (4th ed., pp. 469–482). Newark, DE: International Reading Association.

Anthony, R., Johnson, T., Mickelson, N., & Preece, A. (1991). *Evaluating literacy: A perspective for change.* Portsmouth, NH: Heinemann.

Au, K. (1993). *Literacy instruction in multicultural settings.* Fort Worth, TX: Harcourt Brace Jovanovich.

Barton, J., & Collins, A. (1993). Portfolios in teacher education. *Journal of Teacher Education, 44*(3), 200–209.

Brandt, R. (1991). Time for reflection. *Educational Leadership, 48*(6), 3.

Brandt, R. (1992a). On performance assessment: A conversation with Grant Wiggins. *Educational Leadership, 49*(8), 35–37.

Brandt, R. (1992b). On outcome-based education: A conversation with Bill Spady. *Educational Leadership, 50*(4), 66–70.

Brooks, J.G., & Brooks, M.G. (1993). *In search of understanding: The case for constructivist classrooms.* Alexandria, VA: Association for Supervision and Curriculum Development.

Bruneau, B. (1995). *Studying student work to inform decisions about portfolio assessment in preservice developmental literacy courses.* Paper presented at the 45th Annual Meeting of the National Reading Conference, New Orleans, LA.

Commission on Higher Education. (1996). *Framework for outcomes assessment.* Philadelphia, PA: Middle States Association of Colleges and Schools.

Darling-Hammond, L.D., Ancess, J., & Falk, B. (1995). *Authentic assessment in action: Studies of schools and students at work.* New York: Teachers College Press.

Desai, L.E. (1993). *Portfolio assessment in the pre-service classroom: A plethora of possibilities.* Paper presented at the 43rd Annual Meeting of the National Reading Conference, Charleston, SC.

Dixon-Krauss, L. (1996). *Vygotsky in the classroom: Mediated literacy instruction and assessment.* White Plains, NY: Longman.

Ferrara, S., & McTighe, J. (1992). A process for planning: More thoughtful classroom assessment. In A. Costa, J. Bellanca, & R. Fogarty (Eds.), *If minds matter: A foreword to the future* (Vol. 2). Palantine, IL: Skylight.

Flood, J., & Lapp, D. (1989). Reporting reading progress: A comparison portfolio for parents. *The Reading Teacher, 42,* 508–514.

Flower, L., & Hayes, J.R. (1994). A cognitive process theory of writing. In R.B. Ruddell, M.R. Ruddell, & H. Singer (Eds.), *Theoretical models and processes of reading* (4th ed., pp. 928–995). Newark, DE: International Reading Association.

Ford, M. (1994). *Portfolios and rubrics: Teachers' close encounters with self-evaluation as learners in teacher education courses.* Paper presented at the 44th Annual Meeting of the National Reading Conference, San Diego, CA.

Gellman, E. (1992–1993). The use of portfolios in assessing teacher competence: Measurement issues. *Action in Teacher Education, 14*(4), 39–44.

Graves, D.H. (1990). *Discover your own literacy.* Portsmouth, NH: Heinemann.

Harrison, C. (1996). *Alternative literacy assessments: Have they lived up to their promise?* Paper presented at the 41st Annual Convention of the International Reading Association, New Orleans, LA.

Hart, D. (1994). *Authentic assessment: A handbook for educators.* Menlo Park, CA: Addison-Wesley.

Heiden, D. (1996). *Modeling authentic practice and assessment: Practicing what we preach in reading/language arts methods courses in teacher education.* Institute presented at the 41st Annual Convention of the International Reading Association, New Orleans, LA.

Kaywell, J.F. (1993). *Adolescent literature as a complement to the classics.* Norwood, MA: Christopher-Gordon.

Kieffer, R.D. (December, 1994). Portfolio process and teacher change. *National Reading Research Center News, 8.* publication draft.

King, P.M., & Kitchener, K.S. (1994). *Developing reflective judgment: Understanding and promoting intellectual growth and critical thinking in adolescents and adults.* San Francisco, CA: Jossey-Bass.

Linn, R. (1995). *Assessment-based reform: Challenges to educational measurement.* Presented as the William H. Angoff Memorial Lecture. Princeton, NJ: Educational Testing Service.

Lipson, M.Y., & Wixson, K. (1991). *Assessment and instruction of reading disability.* New York: HarperCollins.

McKinney, M.O., Perkins, P.G., & Jones, W.P. (1995). Evaluating the use of self-assessment portfolios in a literacy methods class. *Reading Research and Instruction, 35*(1), 19–37.

McLaughlin, M. (1986). *Minimum competency testing: A national trend.* Paper presented at the 27th Annual Convention of the International Reading Association, Philadelphia, PA.

McLaughlin, M. (1994). *Literacy histories of preservice teachers: The effect of the past on the present.* Paper presented at the 44th Annual Meeting of the National Reading Conference, San Diego, CA.

McLaughlin, M. (1995). *Performance assessment: A practical guide to implementation.* Boston, MA: Houghton Mifflin.

McLaughlin, M. (in progress). *Creativity in young adult literature: Bringing authors to life.*

McLaughlin, M., & Kennedy, A. (1992). *Pennsylvania's Chapter V revisions: An administrator's guide.* Princeton, NJ: Houghton Mifflin.

McLaughlin, M., & Kennedy, A. (1993). *A classroom guide to performance-based assessment.* Princeton, NJ: Houghton Mifflin.

McLaughlin, M., & Vogt, M.E. (1995). *Performance portfolios for inservice teachers: A collaborative model*. Paper presented at the 45th Annual Meeting of the National Reading Conference, New Orleans, LA.

Merseth, K.K. (1993). How old is the shepherd? *Phi Delta Kappan, 74*(7), 548–554.

Mosenthal, J., Daniels, P., & Mekkelsen, J. (1992). *The portfolio-as-text: Literacy portfolios in preservice, undergraduate, teacher education*. Paper presented at the 42nd Annual Meeting of the National Reading Conference, San Antonio, TX.

National Board for Professional Teaching Standards. (1989). *Toward high and rigorous standards for the teaching profession*. Washington, DC.

Neill, D., & Medina, N. (1989). Standardized testing: Harmful to educational health. *Phi Delta Kappan, 70*(9), 688–702.

Ohlhausen, M. (1994). *Institutional concerns in implementing portfolios in teacher education*. Paper presented at the 44th Annual Meeting of the National Reading Conference, San Diego, CA.

Ohlhausen, M., Perkins, P., & Jones, P. (1993). *Assessing self-assessment portfolios in literacy methods classes*. Paper presented at the 43rd Annual Meeting of the National Reading Conference, Charleston, SC.

Paris, S. (1991). Portfolio assessment for young readers. *The Reading Teacher, 44,* 680–681.

Pearson, P.D. (1994). In M.E. Vogt & M. McLaughlin (Chairs), *Portfolios in teacher education: Issues, implementation, and inquiry*. Symposium conducted at the 44th Annual Meeting of the National Reading Conference, San Diego, CA.

Pikulski, J. (1990). The role of tests in a literacy assessment program. *The Reading Teacher, 43,* 686–688.

Roehler, L. (1995). *Growing and evolving with portfolios*. Paper presented at the 45th Annual Meeting of the National Reading Conference, New Orleans, LA.

Roth, R.A. (1989). Preparing the reflective practitioner: Transforming the apprentice through the dialectic. *Journal of Teacher Education, 40*(2), 31–35.

Ruddell, M.R. (1995). *Literacy history stories: Student teachers' reflections on and understandings of their own literacy development*. Paper presented at the 45th Annual Meeting of the National Reading Conference, New Orleans, LA.

Ruddell, R.B., & Ruddell, M.R. (1995). *Teaching children to read and write: Becoming an influential teacher.* Boston, MA: Allyn & Bacon.

Ruddell, R.B., Ruddell, M.R., & Singer, H. (Eds.), (1994). *Theoretical models and processes of reading* (4th ed.). Newark, DE: International Reading Association.

Rumelhart, D.E. (1994). Toward an interactive model of reading. In R.B. Ruddell, M.R. Ruddell, & H. Singer (Eds.), *Theoretical models and processes of reading* (4th ed., pp. 864–894). Newark, DE: International Reading Association.

Schon, D. (1987). *Educating the reflective practitioner*. San Francisco, CA: Jossey-Bass.

Shepard, L. (1989). Why we need better assessments. *Educational Leadership, 46* (7), 4–9.

Short, K.G., & Burke, C. (1996). Examining our beliefs and practices through inquiry. *Language Arts, 73,* 97–103.

Stowell, L. (1993). *A team approach to portfolios in teacher education*. Paper presented at the 43rd Annual Meeting of the National Reading Conference, Charleston, SC.

Stowell, L.P., & Tierney, R.J. (1995). Portfolios in the classroom: What happens when teachers and students negotiate assessment? In R.L. Allington & S.A. Walmsley (Eds.), *No quick fix: Rethinking literacy programs in America's elementary schools* (pp. 78–94). New York: Teachers College Press; Newark, DE: International Reading Association.

Swafford, J. (1995). "I wish all my groups were like this one": Facilitating peer interaction during group work. *Journal of Reading, 38*, 626–631.

The Pennsylvania State System of Higher Education. (1996). *Shaping a new era for public higher education in Pennsylvania: A vision for the state system*. Harrisburg, PA: State System of Higher Education.

Tierney, R.J. (1996). *Alternative literacy assessments: Are they living up to their promise?* Paper presented at the 41st Annual Convention of the International Reading Association, New Orleans, LA.

Tierney, R.J., Carter, M.A., & Desai, L.E. (1991). *Portfolio assessment in the reading-writing classroom*. Norwood, MA: Christopher-Gordon.

Valencia, S. (1990). A portfolio approach to classroom reading assessment: The whats, whys, and hows. *The Reading Teacher, 43*, 338–340.

Valencia, S.W., Hiebert, E.H., & Afflerbach, P.P. (Eds.). (1994). *Authentic reading assessment: Practices and possibilities*. Newark, DE: International Reading Association.

Viechnicki, K., Barbour, N., Shaklee, B., Rohrer, J., & Ambrose, R. (1993). The impact of portfolio assessment on teacher classroom activities. *Journal of Teacher Education, 44* (5), 371–377.

Vogt, M.E. (1989). *A study of the congruence between preservice teachers' and cooperating teachers' attitudes and practices toward high and low achievers*. Unpublished doctoral dissertation, University of California, Berkeley.

Vogt, M.E. (1994). *Individual goal-setting: Preservice teachers developing the agenda*. Paper presented at the 44th Annual Meeting of the National Reading Conference, San Diego, CA.

Vogt, M.E., & McLaughlin, M. (1995). *Assessment: Issues, trends, and implementation*. Paper presented at the 9th European Reading Conference, Budapest, Hungary.

Vogt, M.E., McLaughlin, M., & Ruddell, M.R. (1993). *Do as I do: Using portfolios to evaluate students in reading methods courses*. Paper presented at the 43rd Annual Meeting of the National Reading Conference, Charleston, SC.

Vygotsky, L.S. (1987). The development of scientific concepts in childhood. In R.W. Rieber & A.S. Carton (Eds.), *The collected works of L.S. Vygotsky. Vol. 1*. New York: Plenum.

Wellington, B. (1991). The promise of reflective practice. *Educational Leadership, 48*(6), 4–5.

Wiggins, G. (1993). Assessment: Authenticity, context, and validity. *Phi Delta Kappan, 75* (3), 200–214.

Winograd, P., Paris, S., & Bridge, C. (1991). Improving the assessment of literacy. *The Reading Teacher, 45*, 108–116.

Wolf, D. (1989). Portfolio assessment: Sampling student work. *Educational Leadership, 46* (7), 35–39.

Wolf, K., Whinery, B., Hagerty, P. (1995). Teaching portfolios and portfolio conversations for teacher educators and teachers. *Action in Teacher Education, 17*(1), 30–39.

Worthen, B. (1993). Critical issues that will determine the future of alternative assessment. *Phi Delta Kappan, 74*(6), 444–454.

Zeichner, K., & Tabachnick, B. (1981). Are the effects of university teacher education "washed out" by school experience? *Journal of Teacher Education, 32*(3), 7–11.

Author Index

SUBJECT INDEX

Note: An "*f*" following a page number indicates that the reference may be found in a figure; a "*t*" indicates that it may be found in a table.

R

S

U

UNIVERSITIES: admission to, 95–96; portfolio development in, 27–28, 99
UNIVERSITY OF CALIFORNIA, SANTA CRUZ, 96

V

VALIDITY, 12, 69–70

W

"WALK THROUGH MEMORY LANE" (STUDENT WORK), 128–134
WORLD CONGRESS, 103
WRITING, 87–88

Y

YOUNG ADULT LITERATURE: family life and, 85–86. *See also* "Teaching Reading Through Young Adult Literature" course
YOUNG AUTHORS' DAY, 46

Z

ZONE OF PROXIMAL DEVELOPMENT, 10